PORN STAR

EVERYTHING YOU WANT TO KNOW
AND ARE
EMBARRASSED TO ASK

Steven St. Croix

End photo credit
Michael Sanville

Acknowledgements

I'd like to thank M.E. in New York for your time and guidance on this little book, J.G. in Los Angeles for your expertise and J.S.J. as well for your support and input on this.

I would also mention a thank you to my friend A.K. for lighting the fire under me to get this done. Park Slope for life bitches!!

I'd also like to thank all the people I've worked with on-camera and hung out with off-camera thru out the years I've been involved in the industry. Some I will never forget and some I can't forget soon enough. To the guys and girls in the business, past and present, I hope you find what you are looking for.

Thanks to all my fans who have watched my work over the years and have been very vocal in their support.

Introduction

My name is Steven St. Croix and I am a porn star.

The lifestyle of the adult performer can seem captivating, sad, or perverse, depending on your point of view. Nevertheless, millions of people are fascinated with pornography and the people in the porn industry itself. They wonder what really happens on the sets of these films and in the business as a whole. In fact, the most searched topics on the Internet today are porn related.

Millions watch it and millions more have questions about what it is like to work as a performer in adult films. Finding answers through mainstream media outlets is nearly impossible. Most of the time, stories regarding the industry are centered only on the money generated by the industry, the moral aspect of pornography, or the ongoing battles with the government prosecution of old obscenity laws. In addition, there are frequent attempts to make the filming, production, distribution and release of adult films extremely difficult and, in some cases, illegal.

What is not often revealed are the inner workings of the industry, how it relates to the people performing in front of the camera, and what really goes on behind the scenes during these film shoots.

-How men and women get into the business

-What it's like to have sex in front of numerous people with someone you may not know well

-The risks involved

-How one makes a career in the industry or fails

-How a typical day on a film set unfolds

-What happens off-screen between the talent

-How the companies view the performers working in these productions

-How a male performer navigates in an industry where women get all the attention

-The mindset needed to perform hundreds of times in less than comfortable settings

Becoming an adult film performer isn't the typical career choice for most people. In today's society, the accepted path to a career involves getting a degree and finding a job in the corporate world that pays well. Performers in the adult industry have always been looked at as rebels; people operating on the margins of society.

Few stop to think of the performers as anything but sex and drug addicts, when in fact, most performers choose to do what they do in order to maintain a standard of living equal to what other white-collar professionals may have.

Whether you are an ardent fan, a casual consumer, or just plain curious, I want this book to give you an honest picture as to what it is really like to be a performer in an industry shrouded by lies, secrecy and misinformation.

My goal is to answer the questions most commonly asked by fans throughout my years in the business. While the questions are framed towards my perspective as a male performer, I've done my best to answer with both sexes in mind.

Thank you for choosing to read the book. I hope you enjoy this and that you find it insightful and honest. I would love to hear your thoughts on the book. You can contact me through my blog site at www.stevenstcroix.com

Table of Contents

EVERYTHING YOU WANT TO KNOW   1
AND ARE   1
EMBARRASSED TO ASK   1

ACKNOWLEDGEMENTS   3

INTRODUCTION   5

CHAPTER 1- HOW DID YOU FIRST GET INTO
THE ADULT BUSINESS?   18

CHAPTER 2- HOW DID YOU KNOW YOU COULD
PERFORM IN THE MOVIES?   27

CHAPTER 3- HOW DID YOU LAND YOUR FIRST
LEAD ROLE IN A FILM?   31

CHAPTER 4- HOW DO YOU KEEP AN ERECTION
THROUGHOUT A SCENE?   36

CHAPTER 5- HAVE YOU EVER NOT FINISHED A
SEX SCENE?   43

CHAPTER 6- WHO ARE YOUR FAVORITE GIRLS
TO WORK WITH?   46

CHAPTER 7- HOW MUCH MONEY DO YOU GET PAID?   52

CHAPTER 8- ARE THERE REALLY "FLUFFERS" ON THE SET TO KEEP A GUY HARD?   57

CHAPTER 9- HOW LONG DO SEX SCENES TAKE TO FILM?   64

CHAPTER 10- DOES THE MAFIA CONTROL THE PORN INDUSTRY?   69

CHAPTER 11- HOW MANY WOMEN TOTAL HAVE YOU HAD SEX WITH IN YOUR LIFETIME?   73

CHAPTER 12- WHAT IS THE MOST NUMBER OF GIRLS YOU'VE HAD SEX WITH AT ONE TIME?   80

CHAPTER 13- HOW DO YOU CONCENTRATE ON PERFORMING WITH SO MANY PEOPLE AROUND?   85

CHAPTER 14- HOW DID YOU GET AN EXCLUSIVE CONTRACT WITH VIVID VIDEO? 92

CHAPTER 15- WHY ARE CERTAIN GIRLS GIVEN CONTRACTS?   99

CHAPTER 16- DO GUYS IN THE FILMS USE VIAGRA?   **105**

CHAPTER 17- HOW MANY DAYS DOES IT TAKE TO FILM A MOVIE?   **113**

CHAPTER 18- WHY DO PORN MOVIES LOOK SO CHEAPLY MADE?   **116**

CHAPTER 19- ARE THE GIRLS AS HOT AS THEY APPEAR ON SCREEN?   **123**

CHAPTER 20- HOW DO YOU CONTROL YOURSELF FROM CUMMING TO SOON?   **129**

CHAPTER 21- DO YOU HAVE A SPECIAL REGIMEN TO KEEP IN SHAPE?   **132**

CHAPTER 22- HOW COME GUYS START OUT IN SHAPE ONLY TO EVENTUALLY GET FAT?   **137**

CHAPTER 23- IS HAVING A BIG COCK REALLY IMPORTANT?   **142**

CHAPTER 24- WHAT DRIVES THE GIRLS CRAZY SEXUALLY?   **149**

CHAPTER 25- DO YOU EVER GET PERFORMANCE ANXIETY?   **153**

CHAPTER 26- HOW OFTEN DO TALENT GET TESTED FOR STD'S? 159

CHAPTER 27- ARE PERFORMERS SCARED OF CONTRACTING HIV? 164

CHAPTER 28- WHY ISN'T THE USE OF CONDOMS MANDATORY? 171

CHAPTER 29- IS DRUG USE PREVALENT IN THE INDUSTRY? 175

CHAPTER 30- DO YOU RECEIVE RESIDUAL PAYMENTS FROM YOUR MOVIES? 179

CHAPTER 31- DO THE GIRLS FAKE THEIR ORGASMS? 182

CHAPTER 32- AREN'T THE GIRLS VICTIMS OF MOLESTATION? 185

CHAPTER 33- WOULD YOU WORK WITH SOMEONE YOU DIDN'T LIKE PERSONALLY? 189

CHAPTER 34- DO YOU DATE THE GIRLS YOU WORK WITH IN FRONT OF THE CAMERA? 195

CHAPTER 35- IS IT TRUE THAT SOME GUYS IN THE INDUSTRY STARTED IN GAY PORN? 198

CHAPTER 36- DOES DOUBLE PENETRATION FEEL STRANGE TO YOU? 201

CHAPTER 37- DO THE GIRLS REALLY ENJOY ANAL SEX? 203

CHAPTER 38- WHAT DO YOU DO IF A GIRL HAS BAD HYGIENE? 206

CHAPTER 39- WHY DO THEY GIVE OUT ACTING AWARDS FOR PORN MOVIES? 209

CHAPTER 40- HOW MANY AWARDS HAVE YOU WON? 212

CHAPTER 41- DO THE AWARDS HAVE ANY MEANING FOR YOU? 214

CHAPTER 42- WILL A PORN ACTRESS HAVE SEX WITH ME OFF-CAMERA? 217

CHAPTER 43- ARE PEOPLE ALLOWED TO VISIT THE PORN SET? 219

CHAPTER 44- SINCE YOU HAVE SEX FOR A LIVING, HOW DO YOU VIEW SEX IN YOUR PERSONAL LIFE? 223

CHAPTER 45- DO THE ACTRESSES WORK AS PROSTITUTES? 226

CHAPTER 46- ARE THE PERFORMERS IN ADULT FILMS SWINGERS?   229

CHAPTER 47- WHAT LEVEL OF EDUCATION DO THE PERFORMERS POSSESS?   234

CHAPTER 48- HOW HARD IS IT TO HAVE A RELATIONSHIP WITH SOMEONE WHO IS NOT IS THE ADULT INDUSTRY?   237

CHAPTER 49- WITH HARDCORE PORN SO PREVALENT, WHY ARE SOFTCORE SEX FILMS STILL BEING PRODUCED?   241

CHAPTER 50- HOW DO YOU FEEL ABOUT BEING RECOGNIZED BY PEOPLE BECAUSE OF YOUR FILMS?   244

CHAPTER 51- DO MALE FANS WANT YOU TO HAVE SEX WITH THEIR WIVES OR GIRLFRIENDS?   247

CHAPTER 52- WOULD YOU ALLOW YOUR KIDS TO GO INTO THE ADULT BUSINESS?   249

CHAPTER 53- WHY ARE PEOPLE LOSING THEIR JOBS AFTER IT'S DISCOVERED THEY HAVE PERFORMED IN ADULT FILMS?   251

CHAPTER 54- DO YOU FEEL THE INDUSTRY HAS EMPOWERED THE WOMAN AS SOME HAVE CLAIMED?   **254**

CHAPTER 55- HOW DOES A PERFORMER CHOOSE THEIR STAGE NAME?   **256**

CHAPTER 56- DO YOU WATCH PORN FILMS?   **259**

CHAPTER 57- DO YOU PREFER REAL BREASTS OR FAKE BREASTS?   **262**

CHAPTER 58- DID YOU BREAK YOUR PENIS?   **266**

CHAPTER 59- DO YOU THINK PORN WILL EVER BE OUTLAWED?   **270**

CHAPTER 60- WHAT FAMOUS CELEBRITIES HAVE YOU MET BECAUSE THEY WERE PORN FANS?   **272**

CHAPTER 61- WHY DIDN'T YOU BECOME A MAINSTREAM ACTOR?   **275**

CHAPTER 62- HOW DO YOU VIEW YOUR CAREER IN ADULT FILMS NOW?   **279**

Chapter 1- How did you first get into the adult business?

In 1991, I was twenty-three and had just moved out to Los Angeles from Miami. I worked different part-time jobs as I was still young and didn't have a clear idea of what exactly I wanted to do with my life. I had made friends with up-and-coming actors and struggling comedians who also worked part-time doing direct phone sales. This enabled them to have their afternoons free for auditions and callbacks. I decided that getting up early in the morning and being done with work by noon or 1pm sounded pretty reasonable. It would give me the rest of the day to do whatever I wanted.

I worked for several companies selling products ranging from office supplies to medical devices. I got bored quickly. I found that I didn't like selling useless shit and I wasn't being challenged in a creative manner. I was inherently a "people person" and doing sales over the phone was stifling. There was one particular job where I was selling B-movies to small video store owners, and the guy sitting across from me mentioned to me how he had once worked for an adult video company selling their videos to independently owned video stores. My ears perked up. That had to be a lucrative business, I thought. I peppered him with questions. I asked him if he knew whether the company would have an opening and whom I should talk to about getting a sales job.

The next day I set up an appointment to go in and talk to a guy named Jerry, who ran the sales staff. We met in person, spoke for a bit, and he offered me a sales position there.

After a few weeks of grinding it out and a particularly difficult couple of days with no sales, Jerry called me into his office. He asked me if I would be interested in making some extra money on the side working as a production assistant for two days on an upcoming film the company would be shooting. The film was the sixth installment of the famous Deep Throat movie. My pockets had been a little light for a few weeks, so I didn't hesitate in asking how much it paid. Jerry told me hundred and fifty per day cash and that, incidentally, his cousin would be directing the movie. As his cousin was stopping by the next morning, I could meet him and ask any further questions I may have.

The next day at the office, in walks Ron Jeremy. I had seen Ron before in videos and knew damn well who he was. Inside, I was pretty excited to be working on my first adult film ever, and the fact it was directed by a legend made me think this could be a sweet gig, maybe with more to come in the future.

Ron and I chatted. He filled me in on the tasks I would be doing and asked if I thought I could handle it. Basically, I would be responsible for feeding the cast and crew, providing clean towels for the talent, and just being an all around gopher-cleaning up the set after scenes and doing anything that needed to be done. I agreed to take the job, and reported to the set a week later.

The first day of filming went smoothly. I met everyone in the cast and crew and was quickly comfortable with my place on the set. It was a trip to see the girls walking around in various stages of undress, totally comfortable with their bodies.

On the second day of filming, we lost one of the actors, "Chad." He had gone off to do a scene in a movie for a different studio and, when he was returning to our set, had been pulled over for speeding, found to have outstanding traffic warrants, and taken to jail.

It was late in the evening on a Sunday and Jerry was worried. He was calling around trying to find someone for the final sex scene to be shot that would have been Chad's scene.

Chad had already been filmed and established in the feature, so if we did find someone, we would have to re-shoot earlier dialogue scenes from the first day with the new actor. But no one was returning Jerry's calls.

Back in 1992, people still used their landline answering machines as a way to get messages from producers pertaining to potential work. While pagers were new and on the market, they were usually only used by doctors and drug dealers. Plus, it was rare that one needed to find a replacement on the very day of a shoot. Most shoots were booked a month in advance.

I pitched an idea to Ron. I could come into the story, introduce myself as an associate of the "Chad" character and do the scene myself. Jerry and Ron thought it could work, and best of all it would mean that we wouldn't have to reshoot any earlier scenes.

The only problem was: I'd never done a porn scene before. And, I needed a test to show that I didn't have HIV. Since the discovery of AIDS, the industry started requiring that the talent get tested before they could work.

I didn't have the document the performers received after testing at a particular facility, but I did have a card from a blood bank where I regularly donated blood. They tested the donations for HIV and when you were clean, they gave you a card showing the time and date you donated and that you were clear. I had been donating for the cash for several months and showed them all the cards I had kept in my wallet.

After some discussion between Ron and Jerry, they explained the problem to the actress and asked her if she would be willing to try working with me. She agreed to give me a chance, and after a little rewriting of the script, they added a character in the film for me to play in order to get the scene finished and the movie done.

As I sat there on set getting ready to film my entrance, I couldn't believe my luck. I was standing there thinking, "I'm going to have sex with a woman on camera in a porn film!!! How cool is this?"

The actress, "Tina," had light blue eyes, porcelain skin and pouty lips. She was lean and very sensuous. She wore a black wig, which made her look like "Aja," the star of the well-known "Squirt Bunny" series at the time.

Surprisingly, I wasn't really nervous. I was rather calm. It was as if I had been waiting for this chance my whole entire life. Since I had the benefit of watching the earlier scenes and seeing the process, I knew what to expect.

We did the dialogue in a few takes and then proceeded to get down to business. As she pulled my cock out for the first time, "Tina" looked up, smiled and said, "Nice cock!" and took me in her mouth.

I thoroughly enjoyed fucking her. I didn't even think about the camera or the crew. I was in the zone. When it was time for the cum shot, I pulled out and came all over her chest. As I cleaned up, "Tina" and the crew each congratulated me for a great scene and being professional.

I was now officially a porn performer.

Chapter 2- How did you know you could perform in the movies?

I never doubted that, if given an opportunity to be in an adult film, I could perform. I sensed that I would be able to focus and not be distracted by people standing around while I was being intimate with a girl. And I definitely wasn't shy about being naked.

You see, I had worked as a male stripper a couple of years prior and spent the better part of a year dancing in front of crowds of women from Miami to Palm Beach. Whatever fear or insecurity I may have had at that time when I began was long gone by the time I was in front of that camera for my first scene.

Being present plays a big part in performing a sex scene in a room full of hot lights, a cameraman sitting a few feet away and a crew member holding a hot light inches away from our junk as we did our thing.

Most people find that once they do something the first time and it goes well, they never have any doubt afterwards. You gain confidence. My biggest fear, when I started, was that the girls would somehow think I was not handsome enough to be in porn. I was twenty-three years old and looked every part of it.

It didn't occur to me that most of the guys in porn films were average looking. Looks weren't so much the first requirement for men. Whether or not one could keep their dick hard was the first concern.

While most girls are worried about how they look in front of the camera, they are far less concerned about the physical looks of their male counterparts. As long as the men weren't scaring animals when they walked down the street, they were acceptable. In fact, many companies shied away from using guys who were deemed too good looking because they usually ended up being prima-donnas. The prevailing thought was that an extremely handsome guy may just be too "into himself" to actually perform well with the girls. When you perform, you have to let go of any vanity you have. And that is a hard task for a lot of guys. Having a personality helps as well.

Performance anxiety never had a chance to take root in my mind. After several successful scenes, having sex on camera quickly became as normal and natural to me as if I were alone in my own bedroom with the girl.

Although my first role had a small amount of dialogue in the scene, it wasn't until my second film that I knew I had what it took to be a significant player in the industry. Within a week of my first scene, I landed my first lead role in a film. By sheer luck.

Chapter 3- How did you land your first lead role in a film?

During a coffee break from my sales job at Arrow Video, I was hanging out and shooting the shit with some crew people next door at the studio where we had shot Deep Throat 6. Arrow owned the space and rented it out to other productions. In the makeup room, there was a public pay phone installed on the wall for people to make and receive calls while working on the set.

This particular morning, it rang and on the other end of the line was a director looking for someone to play the lead role in his film that same day. Apparently, whomever they had hired had cancelled, and he was desperate to find a replacement or the show would be cancelled.

The actor who had answered the pay phone was already booked, so he passed the phone to me thinking I could help with some names.

I spoke to the director and explained I was a new guy who had just performed my first scene for Ron Jeremy's film. He asked me if I was any good with dialogue. I told him it was his lucky day. After getting the address from the director, I asked Jerry if I could leave to do this show. He agreed and an hour and a half later I was on the set.

When I arrived at the house, a bunch of people came out to see who the fuck I was. Mind you, I was unknown AND I had convinced the director over the phone that I would be able to pull off the lead and provide the performance he needed for the movie.

The film was a parody of a popular dating TV show called The Love Connection and they needed someone to mimic the host of the show.

I made my way into the house and met the director along with the various crew and talent. Everyone had been nervously sitting aside that morning, wondering if the shoot would be cancelled because the main role had still not been cast. I received the script, memorized five and a half pages of the opening scene, changed into the suit that I had brought with me and walked onto the set to do a rehearsal for camera and lights. The tension was thick. If I turned out to be someone who forgot his lines or couldn't act, it was going to be a very fucked day for everyone involved, including me.

We ran the lines with the other actors in the scene - minus me actually doing the impression of Chuck Woolery - and we settled to shoot the first take.

I heard, "Roll tape." "Tape speeding," came the reply. "Sound?" someone asked. "Sound speed," came the reply. Then, "Action." It seemed like time slowed down. I launched into my impression of the show host, all the while trying to get the actors to relax with the delivery of their lines and to make it as natural as possible. I could sense some of the crew suppressing giggles while the actor and actress tried to keep straight faces as I hammed it up.

We went through the entire scene; five and a half pages of dialogue; in the first take. When the director yelled, "Cut", I could feel the air rush out of the room in a mass exhalation of relief.

As the cameras repositioned to get the close up shots, the crew was laughing at the scene they just had witnessed and from that point on, everyone involved was confident that not only had the right guy been chosen for the role, but that we were going to finish the movie and have a little fun!

It was in this moment that I realized something. The confidence that led me to convince this director over the phone to hire me for his film - with a budget of $40,000 on the line - this confidence would take me far. Acting on camera came as naturally to me as breathing.

Chapter 4- How do you keep an erection throughout a scene?

Before erectile dysfunction drugs came into existence, keeping your cock hard on camera was all about mental control. That is why you saw only a handful of male performers in almost every movie up into the early 90's.

You may have heard it said that sex is 90% mental and 10% physical. There is truth to that statement. When you think about what it is that makes you interested sexually in someone, it often is your own mind's imagination, your projection of that person. You begin to imagine what their body will look like naked or how they might behave during sex. You imagine what their pussy will look like, how it will taste and smell, and the sounds and expressions that will come out of their mouths during sex. You imagine what the entire sex act will be in your own head.

So, I feel sex is definitely driven by one's mental projection. How many times have you been interested in someone and then, due to a perceived flaw or something they say or do, lose your interest in that person? It is these thoughts that led you to back away.

Maybe you found it difficult to stay aroused because the other person talked too much during sex, was too loud, too easily distracted, or didn't have that certain rhythm you needed to feel connected.

You may have thought the person was "smoking hot" when you first met them, but now you're not so sure you want to fuck them anymore. Your mind plays a huge role when it comes to sex. When I started out in adult films, I would always look for something that I liked about the girl and then focus on that particular thing.

Whether it was her body type, her legs, her feet, her smile, her eyes, or just how she carried herself in person, I would focus on that and let my imagination go. I would imagine what it would be like if there were no cameras at all and it was just she and I, in our own space, where we could have a real connection. Even though we were performing for the camera, most of the time we were enjoying each other sexually.

That was my anchor. That was what kept me hard. I was into the girl. Even when we would stop to catch our breath, wipe off the sweat and have her make-up retouched, I didn't break my mental flow. It was a physical rest but my mind was always active and that was the engine for me. The same was true even when I worked with someone I didn't really connect with.

It may have become difficult to perform with them but the advantage of relying on your mind is that you can make that person become the person you want to be fucking. You can ignore the negative aspects and concentrate on what you do like about them, and that can keep your edge going.

There have been times when I was in a scene with someone and they didn't have the best physical attributes or sexual charisma. Maybe they even had a pitch to their voice that made me want to punch a baby. Whatever it was, if I focused on that one negative thing, it could derail the scene.

So instead, I focused on something positive. Maybe they had great feet or their legs looked awesome in stockings or their nipples were big and erect or they had bewitching eyes. I would concentrate on that part rather than thinking to myself "Jeez, she's got a belly, this sucks," or "The rhythm is off, she doesn't know how to fuck." If they had a great physical part that I liked, then that is what I focused on to get through a scene, if it wasn't going the way I had hoped.

There have also been times when I was so turned on by the girl, that it became a struggle to control myself from cumming too soon. Sometimes, for me, their face and body were too exquisite to look at and control myself. The way their eyes would look at me when we were fucking, the things they whispered in my ear, the way they would move their body to meet my thrusts, the look of ecstasy on their face; all these sensations would lead me to have to pull out and stop for a few minutes in order not to ejaculate.

It wasn't always enough just to pull out, though. Sometimes, the sensations in my cock kept going. There were times when the climax just snuck up on me and all I could hope for was that I could let the cameraman know and that he was pointing the camera at the right place - usually the girl's face or tits.

In Chinatown by Wicked Pictures, my scene with Asia Carrera started with an unplanned ejaculation after the first few strokes in her while she was in a cowgirl position on top of me. If you find a copy, see if you notice the reaction on my face!

Chapter 5- Have you ever not finished a sex scene?

There have been a few times in my career where I could not finish a sex scene no matter how hard I tried. It happens to everyone. We are human and we have problems that get in our way.

In my experience, it usually stemmed from working too much and being burned out sensation-wise. In the first years of my porn career, I worked a lot. Because of my ease with the acting portion of the work, I was working in many story-based porn films. I was also asked to help my fellow cast with rehearsing, to get them to deliver their lines smoothly and as naturally as they could. It takes a lot of energy to be patient, and when you add the long hours on the film set, it can drain your reserves.

I remember one month I had worked 24 days straight. I was so numb from the long days and lack of time to decompress, that I had to stop while in the middle of a scene and tell the director I would not be able to finish. I knew at the time that it would be impossible for me to maintain an erection and to give them a pop shot. I just wasn't feeling it. I had no real sexual desire at that moment. My head was so far away from what I was doing. They ended up having another actor on set do the stunt pop (*). After I went home, it really bothered me.

I was embarrassed by the position I had found myself in, allowing myself to be overworked and having to back out of a scene. I didn't want it to happen again.

I know it sounds odd to say that someone needs downtime from working in porn movies. The time needed to decompress is extremely vital to me. I've had my relationship problems, stupid dramas, family issues, and all the other things that take our energy and attention away from our jobs. But when one is on a set for fourteen hours, performing sex and being frustrated by reciting badly written dialogue, sometimes you just need time to step away and be yourself; hang with your friends and do simple things. Having to be "on" a majority of the time while working on a set takes a tremendous amount of psychic energy. Being in the right headspace is vital for performers when working in porn movies.

*Stunt pop-when someone has to perform the cumshot for another actor because they couldn't pop on cue.

Chapter 6- Who are your favorite girls to work with?

There are many actresses I enjoy working with and some that I had repeatedly asked to be paired up with. Each of them has their different personal and physical traits and I like them all for different reasons.

When I got into the business, most of the stars I knew about were from the late 80's. Women like Barbara Dare, Tori Welles, Porsche Lynn, Amber Lynn and many, many others. For me, they epitomized what a woman should look like and behave like when it came to sex. They were incredibly sexy in the way they carried themselves and the way they performed on screen. It was disappointing for me not to get to work with a lot of them but, as always, there were new girls coming into the business who were pretty and just as eager to be in front of the camera.

In the early 90's the talent pool was small, numbering around 150 people at the most. There were dozens of girls I worked with repeatedly that I enjoyed as partners on-screen and even had the chance to be with offscreen.

The age range of female performers is anywhere between eighteen and thirty-five years of age.

But at the time I got in, the average age of the girls coming into the industry was around twenty-two to twenty-five years of age. I was twenty-three at the time so everyone was either my age or older. There were even a few girls younger than me.

When a girl came into the business at the age of eighteen or nineteen, we would be kind of surprised. Usually, girls who came into the business did so after a few years of being on their own as adults and discovering that they were attracted to the idea of being a porn star-- as opposed to coming out of high school and deciding that porn would be their first choice as a job.

Here are some of my favorites (in no particular order) that I enjoyed working with many times and always tried to be booked with because we had great sex scenes together: Ashlyn Gere, Debi Diamond, Jesse Jane, Asia Carrera, Gina Ryder, Inari Vachs, J.R. Carrington, Kaitlyn Ashley, Lacy Rose, Laura Palmer, Alicia Rio, Nikki Tyler, Racquel Darrian, Melanie Moore, Jenna Jameson, Leanna Heart, Nici Sterling, P.J. Sparxx, Anna Malle, Rebecca Lord, Kira Kenner, Sophie Evans, Sunset Thomas, Tiffany Mynx, Dasha,

Janine, Taylor Hayes, Kayden Kross, Wanda Curtis, Vanessa Chase, Leena, Christina Angel, Roxanne Blaze, Ava Vincent, Avy Scott, Tiffany Million, Sunrise Adams, Sondra Hall, Shy Love, Monique DeMoan, Monique Alexander, Melissa Hill, Monica Mayhem, Julia Ann, Hannah Harper, and Celeste.

Recently, I have worked with a crop of young girls that I like very much. I don't know how long they will last in the business but I request them quite a bit as a performer and a director.

At times, some directors will become infatuated with a new girl solely based on the way she looks in photos. But after shooting them for a video, it becomes very apparent that they didn't perform as well as the director had hoped. This is always a disappointment, because, in the end, all a viewer wants to see is a great sex scene where the chemistry between the performers is real.

Ironically, I have been in scenes that were nominated and won awards that, unbeknownst to many, were actually difficult scenes to get through. Either because there wasn't any connection between the girl and I or the work conditions were not conducive to getting a rhythm.

Scenes that are shot late at night, shot outside in extreme temperatures, scheduled at the end of a long day of shooting, involving a tired crew, or doing crazy positions in places that look great on screen but are nightmares to perform in, all make some of these scenes extremely hard to get through.

But in the end, if the director has enough footage and a good editor, they can end up with a good scene that could get the critic's attention and a favorable mention or an award nomination (*) towards the end of the year.

*A nomination of merit usually is through the AVN, XRCO or XBIZ entities.

Chapter 7- How much money do you get paid?

The business has gone through many peaks and valleys and the pay scale has shifted numerous times from low to high and back down again.

Up until 1987, it was illegal to produce porn in L.A. County, so the pay was much more for those taking the risk to shoot. Most productions paid talent and crew on the same day, or at the end of the shoot. Some even paid with cash in hand.

When I started, the average rate paid to guys was anywhere between $250 and $500 a scene, depending on the type of show it was. If you were someone new, you would be offered a rate closer to the low end. As you became more known and requested by the girls, more directors would cast you in their movies and you could negotiate a higher rate as long as you performed well.

The actresses, however, have traditionally always been paid more. A starting rate of $600 per scene (with no men) would be standard. If the scene was a boy/girl scene, than an offer would be made between $700 and $900. Again, higher demand from the film companies meant higher rates, along with the fact that if the actress was offered the video's box cover (*), she would be paid an additional $500 to $600.

Video companies would then be able to gauge which girls were popular with the viewers by the number of sales and repeat orders from distributors - and they'd make it a point to hire these girls again.

In my early days, an actor would get paid one rate for a sex scene, and an additional rate if they were there most of the day for dialogue. But after several months, I rolled my dialogue rate into my sex scene rate as I felt my time and energy spent on the set substantiated a higher rate.

During my first three years, I was in demand from both directors and certain actresses, and my rate slid up the scale towards $700 a scene.

Eventually, I became known as the go-to guy for roles that required extensive time on screen. I was frequently offered the lead or supporting roles in features. Those roles required that I be on set up to 12 hours or more. If I had a large amount of dialogue, I would be asked to rehearse the scene with the other actors, help the actresses out who may have had difficulties remembering and performing their dialogue, and go to the set to help block out the scene for lighting. Most of the time, I would be on set the entire day for each day of filming, normally two to three days and sometimes upwards of five days.

When I signed my exclusive contract with Vivid Video, we agreed to a rate that broke down to well over $1500 a scene.

My Vivid contract (*) broke new ground for male actors in the industry. We were beginning to be viewed as a valuable asset. Many thought that I charged more because of ego-- but that wasn't the case. I wanted to be paid fairly for my time and talent.

I stood up for myself but wasn't a jerk about it. I feel I helped other male talent who came into the industry after me to make more money.

Over the years, talent raised their rates as they became more aware of how much money the companies were making on various deals. Like corporations, these small companies wanted to earn as much money as possible, while spending as little as they could. The talent, however, wanted fair compensation for their time and energy. They were giving a portion of themselves away on screen, and that footage would be around forever.

*Box cover- what we call the box the videotapes used to be packaged in. They had a photo of the lead actress on the front and stills from the movie on the backside of the box.

*Vivid contract- In 1996, I was the first man to sign an exclusive contract with a video company in the adult business.

Chapter 8- Are there really "fluffers" on the set to keep a guy hard?

Even with the advent of ED drugs, there are performers who still struggle to keep an erection during scenes. The legend of "fluffers" may have gotten its start back in the 70's when there were women on set who just loved sex and may have offered to help a guy keep his edge (*). Whether they were on set as friends of the cast or the producer, or they were bit players in a film, I would surmise that there was a willingness on the woman's part to engage with the male talent, which led to many free blowjobs given on sets that weren't actually filmed.

In porn, it's the guy's responsibility to keep his erection. He's paid very well and frankly, the girls don't want to work any harder just because a guy is having problems with his wood (*).

Plus, some girls actually take it personally if a guy doesn't have a rock hard erection for them right out of the gate. The girls forget that while being attractive certainly helps a guy get hard, most guys like some type of engagement beforehand.

When they fail to realize this fact, it can lead the girls to think that they are not attractive enough, and knowing that some have low self-esteem as it is, this can inflame an already awkward situation, or they start badmouthing the guy to others.

The sex scenes can be long and sometimes arduous, so any extra "work" the girl has to do, is sometimes met with complaints. Imagine having a cock rammed into the back of your throat for ten minutes and then see if you could keep a smile on your face when the guy begins to struggle and is asking for more sucky-sucky.

Now, a girl who is attracted to the guy may not mind offering to help get his edge back, but if a guy begins to get a reputation of needing extra help, it can eliminate future calls for his services.

So, the sad news is, that the legend of a group of girls on set strictly for the purpose of sucking the male talent and helping to maintain their erections is a fairy tale.

That's not to say that many times on set, one can't find the talent sneaking off somewhere for a little personal playtime. There are girls in the industry who do love sex and don't mind fucking and sucking off-camera. Even actresses who only perform girl/girl scenes on camera may actually love dick. I remember one girl, "Angie", who followed me into the bathroom on the set, started sucking me and then took me off to a dark corner somewhere on the set and asked me to fuck her. We had teased each other for months on various sets and finally we were on a set that was sort of relaxed.

I had a scene coming up later in the day and it was the hardest thing to control myself and not cum when I was inside her. She was petite, extremely cute, and had a very tight pussy. We slowly fucked each other for 3 or 4 minutes somewhere in a corner on set. We were getting too hot. Begrudgingly, we stopped and she went off to do her girl/girl scene and I went back to waiting in the green room for my turn to be called on set. Can anyone say blue balls?

Sometimes the energy between performers while working on set becomes too much to resist. There was an instance when I arrived on a set and was scheduled to work with a new Vivid Video contract girl.

As I spoke with her, I realized I had previously seen her in a Rocco Siffredi video entitled Rocco Meats an American in Paris. I was instantly hard. I knew what this girl was capable of, and she was smoking hot, eager and nasty in the video. I had masturbated to her scene at least a dozen times.

Immediately, we were hot for each other and we couldn't wait until our sex scene. We snuck around the house that we were shooting in and found a closet in a vacant bedroom. Immediately the clothes came off and we started fucking. We just wanted a taste of each other.

Again, I had to fight the urge to cum because she was so beautiful and so sexually charged, it was pure bliss to be inside her. Her pussy was so wet and smooth like a pound of soft butter.

When I realized that I was finally fucking this girl that I had fantasized about so many times, it was an unbelievable feeling of satisfaction.

Ironically, I heard she did the same thing with a couple of other actors that were in the film. I guess you could say she was hungry for hog!

*Wood/Edge- another name we call our erections.

Chapter 9- How long do sex scenes take to film?

There are many variables that affect the time in which it takes to shoot a sex scene. However, on average, it's around two hours.

When I started in the industry, the lights used on-set were big and heavy and threw off a lot of heat. This would heat up the sets dramatically and we would have to take several breaks during filming to towel off, cool down, touch up the makeup on the girls and to adjust the lights as the action moved around the set.

Also, the cameras we used in the beginning were big BETACAM cameras - averaging around forty pounds with the bulky battery attached. As they were heavy, cumbersome, and tedious for the cameramen to support on their shoulders for long periods of time, the cameras would initially be set up on tripods for the establishing wide shots, and then taken off and hoisted onto the cameraman's shoulder in order to get the medium and close-up coverage. It was hard work for those guys.

Another factor would be whether or not the director had a clear idea in his head of how he wanted the scene to play out.

Some directors have been editors prior to directing, or worked alongside an editor, so they know what's needed to make the scene work in the movie. However, if the director is unprepared and unsure of what he needs, the scenes can take much longer to shoot, as he will make the cameraman shoot everything on the set from many angles and then try to work it all out later in the editing room. I don't like these types. What we do is not rocket science, so I expect a director to be prepared and know what shots he needs to cut a good movie.

Throughout the filming, we will also stop to let the photographer come in and shoot photos of the different sex positions we have already done and, after the pop shot, he'll come in and shoot stills of that as well. These stills (*) are important, but they also add time to finishing up the scene. Nowadays, some productions will shoot the entire sex scene stills prior to actually filming the scene.

So, when you put all these variables together, the scenes can be shot from beginning to end in two hours. Sometimes, it may take longer, particularly if the guy has wood problems or the actresses heads off for a smoke between shots or is talking non-stop about how cute her dog is. Even as technology changes for the better (the lights don't throw off as much heat, the video cameras are smaller, lighter and easier to work with), it doesn't necessarily make it quicker.

In the end, it just comes down to preparation on the set, an attentive crew, an organized producer and a good director who knows what he wants.

*Stills- what we call the pictures the photographer takes of the actresses for use on the DVD box cover, promotional posters and slicks for distributors.

Chapter 10- Does the Mafia control the porn industry?

Pornography is a billion-dollar industry and everyone seems to have a finger in the pie. Governments, corporate conglomerates and the good old criminal element has always been involved in anything they can derive a profit from, and that especially means the sex industry.

Years ago, when adult films were being shot in New York, many of the films were funded by the mob looking to launder their illegal profits. The peep show booths, videotape stores, and sex shops, along with the theaters themselves, were mostly owned by the mob. While on paper these places were in different names - the mob still owned them.

As the filming moved across the country to the perennially sunny southland of California, so did the mob's reach. Money was kicked back to the families in New York, Chicago, and Philadelphia. The mafia controlled distribution and many films were funded with cash from kickbacks that the distributors gave to the video companies.

Once the monopoly that the Playboy Channel had enjoyed dissipated because of the emergence of The Spice Channel and other adult cable channels, a new avenue for distribution was now available where money could be made without having to deal with the old ways of distribution.

The revenue streams from cable rights, VHS and DVD sales allowed companies to slowly pull away from the influence that the mafia had on the distribution of their films, though some distributors were still having to provide a "taste" up the chain, so to speak.

When the Internet arrived, few could imagine how much of a game changer it would be, including the mob. They tried to muscle in on the new Internet companies, but they were too late. While some of the porn sites that sprang up around the world were being funded, ran, and monitored by the local mob in their respective regions, many more were funded by speculators who had made their fortunes in the dot-com boom. They took their profits and started buying huge amounts of back catalog titles and pictures for the new websites they were starting.

In addition, many of the eastern European girls who flocked into adult films after the fall of the Soviet bloc were controlled and pimped by the mafia's criminal elements in their local regions. Some were able to break free, but many became targets when they returned from the States, some losing everything they had worked for - homes, cars, real estate and other assets- to these mob outfits. Some were charged protection money upon their return, especially if they wanted to buy or remodel a building in a country where property is inexpensive. This protection money made sure that the new construction wasn't gutted by theft of the copper piping, electrical wires and bathtub and toilet fixtures.

While the mafia may not "control" the adult business, they likely have some influence on the industry today.

Chapter 11- How many women total have you had sex with in your lifetime?

Ah. The magic question; how many chicks have I banged? It's odd that men only are really concerned about that. You never really hear girls asking each other, "How many dicks have you taken?" You never see lions on the Serengeti laying around in the shade and discussing how many antelope they've taken down. Have you ever asked a Special Forces guy how many people he's killed?

Somehow, the number of women a man has slept with is supposed to represent how virile he is, what a dick-swinging stud he is. If your good-looking buddy banged 200 girls, you might think he's a god. But you also wouldn't want him dating your sister, would you?

Herein lies the paradox of the issue. Men are supposed to have a high number of conquests. The higher the number, the higher his overall "worldly experience" and the higher his supposed value is in nature.

But in Western countries, where religious doctrines have imposed the belief that a man should, upon reaching adulthood (and his sexual peak) immediately find a "good girl" and settle down and marry. This has led to many, many men actually marrying the first or second woman they've ever slept with! That is crazy!

Of course, on the other side of that coin is the belief that a man who rejects that paradigm and goes out and fucks many woman is by nature immature, holds women with low regard, "uses" women, is selfish or worse yet "preys" on innocent women.

If a woman does the same thing, she's considered a slut, a whore, irresponsible, having low self-esteem or incapable of settling down and becoming a mother.

A girl wants a guy who knows what they are doing in the bedroom. They want a guy who knows how to please a woman. A man wants a girl who is open to all kinds of different sex in the sack; different positions, someone who gives great head, enjoys anal sex, maybe even open to a three way (with another girl!). The dirtier the better! A woman wants a guy who can eat their pussy well, can vary the sex from rough to gentle, knows where to touch them on their body to excite them, knows what to say to them when fucking them.

All these things are what make great sex happen! But in order to be good at it, how is one to find out what works and what doesn't? Be born with an innate skill at it? Hardly. You need to get experience under your belt. You need to go out and fuck. Experience all that sex has to offer, in all of its variety.

The kicker is that when it comes to settling down, we hold that against the other person. We have this crazy idea that there is a specific number range we need to keep our sex partners around. Whether it's 10-30, 30-50, 50-100,100 +; we have a number that to us represents, "Okay that's enough! No more!" And we never tell anyone what this is. We don't even have a basis for this supposed number! As a society, we approach sex with the most outlandish expectations and rules!

I was 18 when I finally got laid for the first time. By the time I started in the business, I had fucked between 300 -350 girls. Why? Because I love girls! They're soft and beautiful and smell good and I like being inside every orifice they have! How did I fuck so many? By asking! By approaching. By making every pretty girl I met know that I wanted to fuck them and by knowing those girls like to fuck as well!

I took certain jobs that I knew would help me meet girls. I did door to door sales. I sold perfume. I worked at a radio station. I worked in retail. I was a male stripper. I went to bars and clubs. I hung out at the beach every day when I lived in Miami. I went to malls. I went to strip clubs. I went where I could meet girls. It didn't hurt that I was tall and considered good looking. But still, I went out and tried to meet girls anywhere and everywhere. When I entered the porn business, I arrived in pussy heaven. I had pussy at work, I had pussy I could take home. I had new pussy always around me. New pussy was coming into the business all the time.

Figuring that 3/5 of the movies I have performed in had me doing two scenes in the movie (sometimes three) and figuring all the movies including one-offs (stand alone scenes or vignettes without a story) that I did, I estimate I have fucked over 1,500 girls total in my lifetime. I've had bad sex, incredible sex, and so-so sex. I believe it has made me quite an experienced lover. I think it has made me attuned to what a woman responds to in bed.

The funny thing out of all this is that I've had women look at me as if I was not "qualified" to be with them. That I was more of a "risk" than the possibility of sleeping with a guy who maybe doesn't even care how to please a women, a guy who just wants to stick his dick in a chick and cum, a guy who has no respect for women, a guy who is physically violent towards women and a man who psychologically abuses women into making themselves feel superior.

Somehow, I had gone above and beyond the "acceptable" number of sex partners. Isn't that crazy?

Chapter 12- What is the most number of girls you've had sex with at one time?

Before films, I pretty much had what one may call an 'abnormal' sex life. Though I was a virgin until a couple months after my eighteenth birthday, I had ended up being with roughly 150 woman by the time I turned twenty-two. I had quite an appetite for girls. But it was always just the girl and I.

My first three-way was with two strippers in Ft. Lauderdale. I was sharing an apartment with one of them at the time and sometimes after work, I would drop by the club where she was and grab a few drinks. That night, she had made a new dancer friend, a gorgeous blonde from Gainesville. After their shift finished, we left together and went back to our place for a night of fun. It was an incredible night for me!

Being alone with two beautiful and hot women and to see them kissing and fucking each other while I was inside either one of them blew my mind. I was twenty-two at the time and I never imagined this would happen to me. But this night, it seemed like it was too easy.

Another awesome three-way I remember was the one I had with Jenna Jameson and Brittany Andrews. Jenna was new in the business at the time and we were having some fun off-camera. One night, I was preparing a little dinner for the two of us; nothing special, just some pasta recipe that was easy to make. Jenna calls and apologizes for being late. She says I'll be very happy when she arrives.

She shows up twenty minutes later with Brittany in tow. Brittany is wearing denim shorts, a pink halter top, cowboy boots, and has a voice like Fran Drescher. The girls don't have an appetite for pasta but they do want sausage. I throw the pasta in the sink and we head straight to the bedroom.

It was pretty amazing for me to have this happen, since I was the new guy in the industry and still wrapping my head around how easily sex with my fellow performers came about off-screen. We were young, horny, and enjoying all the perks of our budding careers. We would just call each other up and then head over to fuck. I loved the 90's!

The most number of girls I've had sex with at one time was in a film from Sin City called The Bachelor. It was a parody of the reality TV show, and in it I fucked Hannah Harper and five other girls. The idea of sex with six girls may sound fun, but the reality is that doing a scene with six girls is much harder than you think. You need to be engaged with as many of them as possible throughout the scene, yet still make it look natural and relaxed.

When my attention is on two or three girls, then the others would play with each other while I proceeded on to the next girl. At that point in my career, it was the most arousing scene I had participated in.

Just seeing six beautiful naked women squirming around, waiting for me to fuck them blew my imagination away. It made me ravenous and turned me into an animal, where I wanted to taste each and every one thoroughly, and fuck them as hard as possible.

Chapter 13- How do you concentrate on performing with so many people around?

Performing sex on camera comes down to mental focus and the ability to not be embarrassed to be seen naked or engaging in sex. You can't focus on the thought that someone may be judging you or your performance. You have to be confident that you are hired to do the job because you excel at it.

Much like when an athlete competes, I get in the "zone." It almost becomes a ritual. I have a belief that I always remember- No one is judging. No one is jealous. We are all here to make the best possible show that we can.

Usually there are six or seven people persons on set watching and working alongside the scene. The director, the cameraman, the tech engineer, the sound guy and his boom operator, a couple of lighting guys, the still photographer and a production assistant round out the crew.

If the budget allows for it, there may be two cameramen filming. One cameraman will record the softcore angles (where you don't see penetration), while the other one gets the hardcore footage.

The director may also dictate which cameramen will cover the wide, medium, and close-up shots. Also, there is a crew person holding a small light we call the C-light (for close-up shots), which is used to give a touch more light to the areas that naturally become shadowed when two bodies are fucking, so that you can see the penetration. In positions like missionary or doggy, the light has to be pointed at the penetration so you can see all that wholesome goodness!

It can be difficult when media and industry writers are invited on set. They will usually sit off on the side, taking notes regarding the scene, the players and the overall production environment. Sometimes, they carry on conversations with the director, crew, or talent that they will thread into their story. Promotion of the movies is extremely vital to the companies, and they want to make sure their shows are being written about and covered in the various magazines and online sites dedicated to the porn business.

There have been occasions when I've had to politely ask that the set be cleared of anyone not essential to the filming of the scene because having so many people on set makes it hard to focus. This gave me a reputation of being difficult at times, but not everyone grasps that it isn't always as easy as it appears to perform a scene. Most of the time the scenes are shot in uncomfortable places and unusual scenarios-- pool tables, staircases, desks, kitchen counters, garages, fireplaces, pianos, on the hood of cars-- and it can be difficult to find a rhythm.

Sometimes it's something as simple as having to be up on the tips of your toes throughout a standing doggy position because the girl is wearing 5 inch heels, her hips are above yours, and you have to try to reach her in order to fuck.

Imagine fucking for ten minutes while
standing on your toes and moving up and down
in a standing doggy position while twisting your

hips out at a 45-degree angle so that the camera can see the penetration. So you're actually fucking in a semi-circular motion. Yeah, that's natural.

Being in a doggy position on top of a pool table or on the floor with no padding is hell on one's kneecaps. Fucking on a couch where the left knee is on the floor while the right knee is up on the couch and maintaining an upright and open position wreaks havoc on one's lower back.

It's not always a given that a scene will be filmed on a comfortable surface, like a couch or a bed. And even then, the beds are so cheap and the springs so worn that you end up sinking in the middle of the bed and being swallowed up like the scene from Friday the 13th. That can really throw your rhythm off, because you constantly have to readjust and make it possible for the camera to see the proper coverage.

The unspoken mantra on the set is: "If it's comfortable, it's boring." The business is about selling the fantasy- that sex happens anywhere, anytime, and under any circumstance. Next time you watch a movie, if the scene looks like it would be totally ridiculous and uncomfortable to do in real life, then it most likely was ridiculous and uncomfortable for the performers as well.

Chapter 14- How did you get an exclusive contract with Vivid Video?

Within my first two years in the industry, I quickly established myself as a reliable and competent performer amongst the companies who sold their movies to the cable channels Spice and Playboy. In order to receive a deal, the channels required that the movies they broadcast required a storyline and a pretty cast of performers who could perform the roles in a passable manner. These films were targeted at the couples market, where both sexes could watch the film without it being too heavily geared towards the male perspective of sex. I was chosen for lead roles because of my ease with the acting portion of the work, in addition to my sex performance in scenes.

Vivid Video had an exclusive cable deal with Playboy, and it was important to them that they have strong actors in their films. Within four months of my first lead role, an actor named Jonathan Morgan introduced me to Vivid Video directors Paul Thomas and Bud Lee. Jonathan and I had quickly become friends and acted in several movies opposite each other. Up until me, he had been the last male performer to come into the business who was adept at comedic roles.

Whereas videotape had become the standard format for shooting porn, Paul Thomas was one of the few directors who still shot on 16mm film.

His films tended to explore the dramatic elements between people in the story and were based on feature-length scripts, heavy with plot development and dialogue.

When he cast me in my first leading role for Vivid in the film Blindspot with Lene Hefner, he mentioned in passing how great it would be to have an actor always at the ready for him and the company. Unbeknownst to me, Bud and Paul had approached the CEO of Vivid Video, Steve Hirsch, proposing that he sign myself and another actor to the company, so they would always have an actor of their choice to cast in the lead male roles. At the time, Mr. Hirsch wasn't convinced that it would be worth anything to the company, and nothing came out of the discussion.

Due to the expanding cable deal Vivid had with the Playboy Channel, the number of productions increased and I ended up working in many Vivid movies. Towards the end of 1995 and after some reconsideration, Steve Hirsch offered me an exclusive contract with the company for the following year.

Steve Hirsch asked my opinion regarding who the company should bring in and sign, so that it wasn't just me in every single title. I suggested Jon Dough. He was a veteran actor, good looking, a little older and his on-screen style contrasted mine. Steven agreed. It would be a good balance.

I was pretty fucking excited to have a contract. Vivid was the top of the mountain in some terms. They received the most exposure and they had a roster of the most beautiful girls signed to contracts.

To be thought of as worthy of a contract and being the first guy signed in an industry where the girls get most of the attention, made me feel like I had cemented my place in adult film history. It also meant that I wouldn't need to constantly find the next jobs to book. While I was very good at socializing and reaching out to people I hadn't worked with before, it was a bit of stress that I was glad to let go off.

Jon and I became the only two guys to be under contact in the porn business. And later that year, Vivid's big film Bad Wives was nominated for sixteen AVN Awards. He and I earned several nominations, along with other cast members and we swept the top categories in which we were nominated for, and we got several nods for the other cast members as well. This film is on the list of AVN's Top 20 All Time Best Porn Films.

After our success, some companies tried copying the same model by signing male performers to their roster but none had the success that Vivid Video received.

Chapter 15- Why are certain girls given contracts?

In any industry, there are people who are at the top, the middle and the bottom. The porn business is not any different. There are people who come along and because of their looks and their energy, stand out from the rest.

The point in having a performer under contract is to assure that they are under exclusive control of the company and that they can benefit from someone's popularity among the fans. Usually, this was reserved for really beautiful girls who came into the business. Most of the time they were knockouts. If you look at the quality of girls that Vivid had signed, you would find that they were distinct looking and had great bodies. Girls like Janine, Tori Welles,

Racquel Darrian, Taylor Hayes, Jenna Jameson and Chasey Lain were exotic looking women who came into the adult business during a time when other girls were pretty but not unique looking.

Now, if you (as a company) were to come across someone who is exotic looking, you want to control the amount of content that is available so as to milk their popularity and extend your company earnings. Control the supply and you control the market. So it behooves one to find a girl that no one else has shot or at least has very little content available.

Then you slowly release their movies over an extended period of time hoping that the fans will stay loyal to the girl as long as she looks great and more importantly does phenomenal scenes.

The paradox is this. In order to build a big fan base, you need to work a lot and have a certain amount of films available to the viewers. But if you have too many films out, there won't be any incentive for the fans to continue to follow you especially if you are not releasing as many titles as before now that the girl is under contract. If you turn the water faucet down too much, people will move on to where they can find an abundant supply of water elsewhere.

There is a tipping point where too much or too little can backfire or work to the advantage of the company. The old model was to have the girl maybe do some girl/girl scenes first. Then you would have her do her first boy/girl scene. After which you would add a few different guys to her roster that she liked working with so that the viewer can see her respond differently to how these guys fuck them.

Then, you would have her do her first anal scenes with some guys and hopefully one of them would be Rocco Siffredi and his big hog of a cock. Later, you would have her do a double penetration scene, an orgy scene or even a gangbang. Lastly, you would have her do an interracial scene.

This model allowed the company to manipulate the perceived "sexual journey of the girl" from sweet and innocent to sexually depraved cock monger slut.

This seemed to be how a man's mind used to work. There was an interest in how a woman sexually awakens. Now, that model is dead.

Today, you have the cutest youngest girls getting fucked up the ass by huge guys in gangbangs. These girls do everything all at once. Instead of measuring it out over the long haul, they allow themselves to get booked everyday until everyone in the industry has shot them and they've done everything imaginable on camera. Then they get pushed aside for the next cute girl who comes along and the cycle continues. We call it "shot out."

This is one of the reasons why there are fewer contract stars anymore. There is no interest in the long tail business. There is little concern over the career of the girl especially when they seem to want to quit every 6 weeks because of boyfriend problems. It's a "here now, gone tomorrow" attitude that has infiltrated itself into the minds of many people in the industry as they fight for the last scraps of a morphing industry.

With a large majority of porn being about degradation and humiliation of the female, many girls don't realize that debasing themselves so quickly in doing all these various forms of sex doesn't make for a long career. Before, there was a status and class to being under contract and if in the right hands, you could establish yourself as an icon for the time being. It seems now that the girls last about as long as an ice cream cone does in the hot summer sun.

Chapter 16- Do guys in the films use Viagra?

When I first came into the business, I discovered that some of the male actors had what they swore to be their "one true concoction" for guaranteeing a good edge for a scene. Some swore that eating lots of protein would have them maintaining wood and shooting large loads. These guys also worked out and took their physical appearance seriously. Others had different concoctions of more natural things to take before scenes. Peter North swore by fresh pineapple. I found that a mixture of ginseng extract and yohimbe bark worked well for me. My experience was that the ginseng allowed me to ejaculate with more volume, and the yohimbe hit me like a good shot of espresso.

But that was the extent of it. Many guys preferred getting stoned before their scene, as it relaxed them and gave them a sort of "tunnel vision" where they were focused only on the girl and other distractions could be ignored.

After Viagra, Levitra and Cialis were introduced to the public, some guys in the industry became scared that any fucking douchebag could come in and do what we did - and take work away from us. So, some started taking these dick pills. Unfortunately, the newer guys who came into the business in recent years have relied too heavily on these pills and I believe it led to the quality of scenes declining.

These guys go out and party all night and figure they can just show up on set, pop a pill and their dick will work. But there isn't any connection between the performers. You don't see the lust, the hunger in the eyes- the excitement of fucking a new person. All these elements stem from the mind of a person who is engaged in the moment.

For me, it has always been about the mental state that I get myself into. A majority of the time, that is all I need. There are times when I struggle, either because of personal issues going on in my life, or perhaps I have worked with the girl so often that it becomes little stale for me. Having a variety in sex partners is wired into our DNA.

Soon, guys started relying on the pills all the time (*). Their thinking was, "as long as my dick is hard, it will be a good scene." They would disconnect from the girl entirely and rely on this pill to carry them through the scene. Don't get me wrong, it was always great to have it in case of a weak libido, but it seems that guys are so afraid of the risk of a weak performance that they gobble them like Skittles. But no one expects perfection every time. That would be the same as expecting a baseball player to hit a home run every time he walks up to the plate.

When these pills first came out, we would whisper among ourselves about whom we thought was taking them. It was often obvious, as some of these guys would show the outward signs of flush skin and a remarkable ability to stay rock hard even when we weren't filming. If someone were to yell "Fire!" in the studio, they would still have a hard-on as we all ran outside. But most looked at the pills as a solution for weaker performers, and it showed when guys who were known for being "hit or miss" started having rock hard erections in every scene.

It is now generally a non-issue if male talent takes a pill prior to a scene. But in my opinion, a hard cock doesn't equal a hot scene. You still need to have some passion, some connection with your partner. These guys become circus monkeys; going through the positions and motions but without an ounce of connection in their souls.

But this widespread acceptance of dick pills, suddenly meant that any guy could come in with a hard dick and have sex in front of the camera. And when that happened, porn went from an industry of professionals to an industry littered with amateurs. At the end of the day, that was all that these guys brought to the table; no charisma, no personality, no charm; just a hard cock and the vocabulary of a goat.

It takes a professional to maintain his edge around a crew of 8 to 10 people, with lights being rigged, constant starting and stopping, technical issues and whatever else he may encounter. It takes a professional to be patient with the process of making a film. You have to keep in mind that these films are about sex. And with a sex scene taking up to two hours to shoot, and with up to seven of them in a film, you can see why guys need to be sharp. If you were a weak performer, you would end up costing the show money through delays and overtime, and nobody wants to be waiting around for a guy to struggle through his scene.

Anyone can fuck a girl in front of a guy holding a small camera and a PA in the background. When you are involved in a feature with a multi-day schedule and time issues, it is the real deal, and many cannot handle the responsibility or pressure. That is the difference between a professional and an amateur.

* Some guys use Caverject, which is injectable directly into the penis.

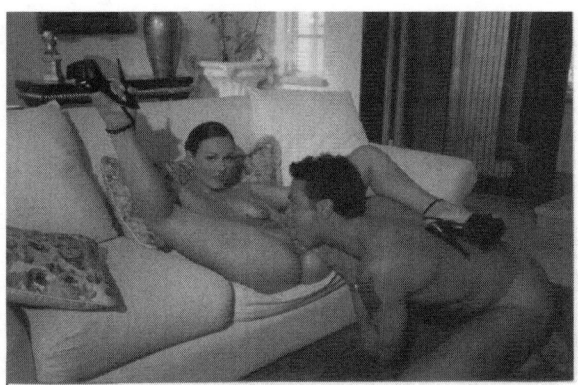

Chapter 17- How many days does it take to film a movie?

Filming a porn movie takes about two to three days, on average. Budgets vary from project to project; some larger budgets allow for a week of filming, while smaller ones give you only a day. When I started, many of the films were budgeted between $30,000 and $40,000 as the prices for adult titled videotapes retailed between $60 and $70 apiece, a profit could easily be made.

The blockbuster film Pirates starring Jessie Jane took around two weeks to shoot, and then another two to three months for visual effects to be completed. I would say that film cost about

$200,000 before special effects. That is one of the rare films that came along and defy the notion that an expensive adult film can't make money. That film made a lot of money!

Eventually the retail price for video and DVD fell. The budgets seemed to shrivel up and the days we worked to complete the film became longer. This forced the more ambitious directors to shoot in 16 to 20 hour days, sometimes back to back shooting days. We hate these productions because it's unsafe. It's bad for morale and it forces many cast and crewmembers to drive home late at night or early into the morning, extremely tired and prone to accidents.

Of course, if they are booked on another show, it fucks up that show as well as everyone is tired and the talent looks like crap. No one gets the sleep they need and everyone is sour because of having been on the previous set for extremely long days.

Chapter 18- Why do porn movies look so cheaply made?

Adult films have always had much lower budgets than TV shows and studio films. The budgets for these productions are in the millions of dollars, while ours are generally in the tens of thousands. But because we have become accustomed to seeing more and more movies and TV shows, our eyes can recognize that there is a huge difference in quality.

There was a time when one could shoot an adult film for 60k to 100k and still make money. The cost of film stock, camera rentals, costumes, lavish sets, and locations while using a proper film crew made making the best film you can a priority. Once you transferred the film to videotape, they would sell for $60 or $70 a piece. There was a lot of money made in porn in the early years.

But cable TV came into the picture, sex film theaters closed, VHS tapes became cheaper to buy, and the profit margins shrunk. On top of that, the days of renting out a small office and paying people under the table ended. Now companies were on the Treasury Department's radar and had to file taxes like everyone else. Business taxes, payroll taxes, unemployment, Social Security, FICA, etc, etc- you get the picture. It became costly to run a business. So what's the natural progression in trying to save money? Pay less for the movies. Less for the cast, less for the crew, less for locations, less for food, blah, blah, blah.

Slowly, the budgets for adult films became smaller. The cost of shooting on film was much higher than recording straight to tape. Shooting on film became a luxury that few companies could afford.

Film looked better than video but video was the cheapest way to shoot and still expect a decent return on the investment. So companies shot on videotape. Tape quality along with the camera's ability to record good pictures was in its infancy. HD wasn't even a dream yet.

Over time, the medium for delivery of adult films changed from tape to DVD. The costs to the consumer dropped as well, because manufacturing costs were lower.

It became cheap to burn these titles onto a DVD disc but the same profit margin enjoyed in the past wasn't sustainable. Smaller returns and smaller budgets meant lower quality films. The reason these movies look cheap is because of the small budgets, and the fact that many of these were shot in a couple of days, on sets, because renting a real location was too expensive. The sets are decorated with a minimum amount of design and used over and over again by the companies that rent the studio space. There is less emphasis on the art of making erotic films anymore. The movies have only become a commodity now-- like cheap socks.

Now the business model is collapsing due to the explosion of free and pirated Internet porn. You used to have to come out to California if you wanted to enter the porn business.

It appears that anyone with a camera can film two people having sex, post it on the Internet, and then charge a fee to access the content. All around the world, there is porn being shot and uploaded.

Because of this easy access, there is little motivation to do anything more than to just film the sex. Why spend more money than the other guys when they seem to be selling as much content, if not more than your product and at a lower cost?

Some believe there is no need for an elaborate premise or even a story because they think the only viewers are guys at home on their computer who only needs to see 6 minutes of sex before he's done and moves on with his day. And they may be right.

Many companies are getting feedback from their Internet people or satellite buyers who say "This type of title is selling more than this feature title." Most who view porn realize the acting is so bad, they ask, "Why would I want to watch this? I want to fast forward to the good stuff!"

Porn has become the coke dealer that you call late at night when you've had a bit to drink. You call three dealers and hope one will come through so that you can satisfy your lust for nose candy. It's a fleeting moment; one that you will either regret or think nothing of the next day; and because you just want to get high, you really aren't concerned about the quality. You just want that burn and drip.

But there are other consumers out there with different tastes and while it seems, at the moment, to be a large number of them who are tired of the low quality shit out there and are looking for better porn, they make up a smaller portion of the market. Yes, they are responding to movies that reflect a real effort by the director, better writing and performances of the cast.

But given the current economic climate, many companies cannot afford to diversify their content to appeal to both types of consumers. Thus, if they are making low quality shit and it's selling for them, they will continue to make it.

Chapter 19- Are the girls as hot as they appear on screen?

I heard a joke when I was a kid. It goes something like this.

A man sits in his living room watching a football game on TV. His wife saunters in, stands in front of him with her hands on her hips and asks, "Honey, does this dress make me look big?"

He replies, "Compared to the house?"

Yeah, I know it's dumb. The point is everything is relative. One person's definition of "hot" can be another's "not!"

Have you have ever seen pictures of a famous actress or model during her downtime in some Hollywood gossip rag or website? Without their makeup they are usually average looking. The glammed up version you see in a film is the result of great makeup artists, hair stylists, expert wardrobe people, a top DP along with the key grip who communicate the DP's lighting needs for a particular scene with the electrical department and the director. You're seeing the perfect package, the result of many talented people's work.

When you see them outside of that environment, they are unremarkable; some surprisingly even have bad skin. The same is true for the girls in the adult business. They are quite ordinary looking at first glance. Other than maybe having a curvy body--large breasts and a nice rear-- they are as normal looking in person as most other normally fit people. Usually, it's the diehard fans that recognize these girls when they're out in public. They hardly ever dress up, especially in anything you may see them wearing in videos. That is unless you catch them coming to and from the set. Instead, they wear sweats, comfortable t-shirts and UGGS. With a really capable makeup person, the right lingerie and clothing, proper lighting and an extremely good photographer, these girls can often look beautiful. And that's before post-processing the images.

High definition video is far less forgiving. Nowadays, the cameras pick up every little mole, scar, zit, stretch mark, sunspot and freckle. Nobody's body is perfect. But they are not runway models. They're porn girls. Pretty enough to be called for work and fucked like hell. They're not selling beauty or even femininity. They're selling the fantasy of the slut/whore; the girl that's down to fuck and doesn't really care who it is. Many of the girls on their off days smoke weed and eat garbage food and drink like sailors. They are lucky in that their youth sometimes prevents them from looking like their mothers and sisters back in the tiny little towns of the Midwest. But some girls slowly (or quickly) gain weight and until someone refuses to shoot them, they usually don't do anything about their bodies.

With that said, some workout and have awesome bodies with low body fat and great skin. In the early 90's, Racquel Darrian, Christina Angel, Janine and Leena were just some of these rare types. They had flawless bodies and distinct faces, beautiful legs and tan skin. They looked exactly like they did on film.

Sadly, many of the girls that are working now, have had bad plastic surgery and seem to strive for the "Barbie Doll/Daffy Duck" look, big breasts and fat, pouty lips that look like tire irons were inserted into their lips. Many even try to look like some celebrity that they want to be so badly. In the rush to look like a "hot babe", these girls find the cheapest doctors to do breast enhancements and facial work and then return to work in front of the camera much sooner than recommended. Greedy agents and lazy boyfriends complain to them that they are 'losing money' the longer a girl is recuperating and guilt them into returning to work before they have had the proper time to heal.

Makeup can do wonders but in the end these actresses usually are at least pretty when they come into the business. Unfortunately, many have issues with their looks and feel inferior to naturally pretty girls in the business. Meals made up of healthy food used to be catered on set but now, since the food on set is usually fast food, the girls put on weight rather quickly, thus losing their good bodies. This leads them to make more devastating choices such as liposuction that sometimes cannot be undone in the years after their augmentations.

What you see on the screen is the result of a lot of time and effort made to create the "perfect look" or sometimes a lackluster effort from those shooting the videos in order to get by with the minimum effort.

Chapter 20- How do you control yourself from cumming to soon?

It's really all about the mental game. Physically, I can allow myself to get to that point where I am close to cumming and then back off and disconnect myself from the physical pleasure. But it requires strong will. Even though we are on a film set to work and sometimes it can be uncomfortable, most of us enjoy the sex. However, during the shoot, there is a lot of starting and stopping, which helps establish a certain rhythm to gauge oneself as to how close or far away (from cumming) one needs to be before the pop. I don't worry so much about cumming before they need me to. That is unless; I'm really excited and turned on by the girl! There is always a little part somewhere in my lizard brain that can't believe I get to fuck such slutty hot girls.

I remember the first time I worked with Asia Carrera. It was on a set for a movie called Chinatown and she looked stunning. Asia was tall and shapely with big beautiful round eyes. She looked to be half white and half Asian. I was so excited to be fucking her that when we finished shooting the beginning of our sex scene - the mandatory 'guy gets head, girl gets pussy eaten' part -we moved into our first sex position (cowgirl) and within a minute of entering her, I felt myself starting to lose control and had to pull out and ejaculate.

Her pussy was wet, warm and tight and she looked so sexy looking down at me, that it was much too much for me to control myself. The only thing that saved the scene from being a disaster for me was that I had indicated to the cameraman that I was losing control and about to cum, which gave him time to reset his frame and to get the cumshot on tape. We ended up shooting the scene out of sequence. I still had my boner but I needed some time to refresh my load in case the pop hadn't seen sufficiently and I needed to do another one.

Most of the time, supreme self-control carries me through. But there are times when the girl is so gorgeous and the physical aspect so pleasurable that I don't want to fight any longer and I just let myself go.

Chapter 21- Do you have a special regimen to keep in shape?

Fucking on camera requires two things; a strong back and good lungs. I've always had a strong back from doing pull-ups since my teens and now I've added bridges to my regimen. So many guys have back problems nowadays; slipped discs and muscle spasms. It's primarily from going through our lives sitting all the time and the bad posture when we are sitting. We sit when we drive, sit at our office jobs, sit when we eat. The only time some people walk is to get to the next spot they're going to sit down in.

Good lungs are important. You have to get oxygen to the brain and to your cock. Having smoked 20 years, I don't have the best lungs though I have always been active and exercised.

I've also put on 25-30 lbs of muscle on my frame since I started in films.

When I started, I was a skinny 176 lbs. and 23 years of age. Relying on my youthful metabolism and occasional calisthenics here and there, I didn't need any special workout.

My first year in the business, I started weight training in the gym and taking supplements to get bigger muscles because I thought that was what the girls wanted; big muscular dudes. But I would work out for a month or so, see results and then slack off. I would then return to the gym when I thought I was looking soft.

As far as diet was concerned, I never watched what I ate. I had a fast metabolism and I could eat whatever I wanted. Now, I am very selective of what I eat; mostly vegetables, high quality protein from legumes or fish and a glass or two of wine nightly. I drink distilled liquor on rare occasions.

Some have claimed that eating more protein-based foods would give you better 'loads'. Peter North swore by eating pineapple to get his famous pops but he also was in the gym almost every day. If you've seen his films, you will know he had an incredible physique. I myself took ginseng on the day of my scenes as I thought it made a difference. I don't know if it was more of a placebo effect or what. Staying hydrated and active helped to keep my system ready for the long days on sets. I don't think there is a need for anything more than that. What I eat makes a difference though. Junk food is crap food. It makes your sweat and sperm stink and makes you lethargic. All the oils and saturated fats cling to your heart and waistline.

As long as I wasn't pounding huge amounts of fast food or alcohol, I never had to worry. The biggest factor was getting cardiovascular exercise in between the days of working. I disliked running for a long time but it is the best way to stay lean and develop lung power for those long scenes in front of the camera.

Now, I mostly do circuit training with heavy weights, compound movements and interval running. I mix in some boxing, swimming and an occasional hike up in the hills overlooking Hollywood or Malibu. I feel I look better now than I did 20 years ago.

Chapter 22- How come guys start out in shape only to eventually get fat?

While this business is about keeping your wood first, looks are a close second. When I came into the business, there were only a handful of guys that worked all the time. While they may have been average looking, they had the ability to maintain their erections while filming movies. That's why you will see the same few faces all the time in older porn movies.

There were always new guys looking to enter into the industry. When your young, good looking and plowing a lot of pussy, it seems like the natural progression to try and find your way into porn. In California, working out in the gym is a normal activity; almost required by some unknown state law. Of the new guys who entered, some were male revue dancers and handsome but were also wrapped up in steroids and recreational drug use. After several months in front of the camera, many eventually had problems performing and would fade away from the industry. Sometimes it was because of their excessive life style. For others, it was a mental block that prevented them from continuing. They would meet a girl and fall in love and quit porn because that was what the girl wanted from them to prove their love.

When you're young, you realize that to be considered a "player", you have to look the part. In our culture, there is no doubt that there is more value attached to outward appearances than being a fully developed person, with class, charisma and personality. Obviously, if you look good and are in shape, you would be considered and maybe permitted to get into the industry, provided you performed well.

My advantage when I started was that I was better equipped than most at shouldering the responsibility of being a "star". I was more comfortable acting and reciting dialogue than most of the other male talent. This was very important to the companies that were making porn films with stories, plots and a growing audience of female viewers. To be honest, once I was working regularly and earning good money, I let myself slack off as I enjoyed my new life of relative ease. An influx of money, eating out in restaurants all the time, and late nights out in bars all led to guys putting on a few pounds and not hitting the gym. I think when most people move up in income levels, they experience the same shift. You get comfortable and lazy. We tend to take the path of least resistance. It's in our nature to be comfortable. You are hungry only until you are satisfied.

Male porn stars like Peter North, Mark Davis, TT Boy, Vince Voyeur, Dale DaBone and Nick Manning were handsome and fit. Some continued to workout like madmen while others fluctuated. I was never the gym-guy for very long. I would see progress in a few weeks and then slack off. I relied on the fact that as long as my cock worked and I was performing the acting portion well, I could just maintain.

Porn becomes a lifestyle once you're established. You've "made it". People know your name and your phone rings. They like you and like working with you. Just as when a girl gains ten pounds and is forgiven, so are you. You go out more. Most of us are unhappy in failed relationships and insecurity creeps up and drives us to destructive behaviors. Over time, though, the constant partying catches up with people. Drugs and drinking along with just getting older and one's metabolism slowing down, makes it hard to maintain the shape you were in when you are younger. Easy money and constant dining in restaurants enhance the problem.

A lot of the more recent guys resort to HGH and steroids to maintain their physiques. They get addicted to new fitness crazes like MMA or CrossFit. But eventually some of us get lazy because we're comfortable and don't worry about losing work. That is, until we start losing work because there is a younger, fitter guy that the girls want to work with.

Chapter 23- Is having a big cock really important?

Our culture's obsession with cock size is amusing. It has always been a sign of alpha male dominance and virility throughout centuries. Big cock equals big man. Or so most think. While that may be the case, it's not always a good thing.

I can tell you that many guys in the business that have enormous cocks have confided that they didn't have a lot of conquests prior to getting into porn. While this isn't to say that they didn't have girls interested in them, I do know that when these guys pulled their shit out, many girls freaked out and didn't want anything to do with it. Of course, many woman say that they want a big dick guy to ravage them, but when it comes down to actually doing it, they balk; and with good reason.

First, big cocks hurt them. The average depth of a woman's vagina is six inches. Yes, they stretch out a little bit when they're excited and getting pounded but that happens after some prolonged action. Second, unless they are truly wet; not wet from saliva but truly wet from vaginal secretions; a big fat long cock stretches their opening and hurts. The penetration alone can cause micro tears around the pussy. On top of that, there is the cervix bone at the end of their vaginal cavity. Any cock longer than six inches and straight will most likely hit their cervix bone. Repeated pounding into that bone hurts them and hurts us guys as well.

If you're lucky enough to have a slight curvature to your cock that slides past the cervix bone, then it's not as painful for them.

Since the explosion of Internet porn, it seems that there are more guys out in the real world with big cocks. It seems that they have won the genetic lottery. Maybe and maybe not. Again, while I love to see a petite girl getting ravaged by a big thick cock in her asshole, for me it's only for entertainment value. I love watching Rocco Siffredi crack open these girls on video with his tool. Our mental makeup as guys is to ravage our conquests and to "impale" them with our dicks. We like seeing girls giving up control and "taking" us into the deep extremities of their bodies. Visually, there is probably nothing more arousing, at least for me.

But knowing how to use your cock is just as important! It would be the same as being given a Ferrari to drive. Would you have as much fun in a Ferrari if you only drove it thirty miles and hour for a quarter mile? Hell no! You'd be bored out of your mind and sorely disappointed. You want to experience it going zero to sixty in a flash, braking hard, taking tight corners and power sliding along the road. You want to hear the roar of the engine behind your head, the vibrations of the road, the smell of the tires burning on the pavement and the brakes working overtime to slow down, the sound of the car as it twists and turns to the g-forces of racing in a canyon in the Swiss Alps. That's when you would truly be satisfied with your experience in the Ferrari. Getting out of the car, you would admire the lines and color of this beautiful racing machine. You would be satisfied that you experienced this wonderful piece of craftsmanship in the way it was meant to be experienced.

The same goes for guys. You can't rely on just your dick to satisfy a girl. It's the whole experience. You have to be charming, smooth, rugged, manly, a good conversationalist, someone with some knowledge of the world and not just of your immediate environment. You have to be able to speak about worldly things like history, politics, philosophy and socio-economics. Not that these are things you will be talking about in bed but because these are the things that can open doors to woman deciding that they want to fuck you.

You have to be able to know how to look at a woman, where to touch her on her body, how to calibrate yourself so as to get the best response from her. You need to know how to manipulate her body and guide her through the positions you know she will enjoy and know when to do that. You need to know what to say to her while fucking her and when to say it; or when to say nothing at all. You need to know how to use your own body's scent to your advantage; letting your pheromones do the work nature intended it. You need to now how to regulate your rhythm while fucking so you can prolong her pleasure without being totally selfish and enhance the impact of your body being inside hers.

In short, you have to be that beautiful Ferrari; the whole experience; not just the throttle. Yes, if you won the genetic lottery and have a bigger than normal cock, be grateful but don't let it be what you are only about. Unless you have a three inch penis, the penis you have works just fine. Stop worrying about it and work on being a well rounded person with something of value to offer. That will last longer and have more value than an appendage between your legs.

Chapter 24- What drives the girls crazy sexually?

That's a difficult question to answer. One may assume that what they see on the screen is real but they have to remember that these girls are performing for the camera. Whether or not they are really enjoying themselves can always be called into question, especially when the purpose of the films is to sell the fantasy of sex.

I tend to think many guys don't take the time to slow down and explore the women they're with sexually. When they rush through the beginning and are only concerned with getting their dick wet, then that can lead to many girls not having really experienced the kind of sex where their senses are stimulated to the maximum. Unfortunately, a lot of young guys mimic what they see in porn films and think that is what sex is all about-bang, bang, bang at one speed as hard as you can and then cum on the girl's face. It leaves many girls unfulfilled. And girls do the same as well.

So, when they do end up working with someone who slows down, takes their time and enjoys exploring their bodies, this gets them excited beyond belief and gives them real pleasure they may never have felt before. My goal is to find what they positively respond to and then utilize that during my scene.

Now, with that said, there are girls that just want to be hurt. They want to feel like a truck hit them and they can't walk right for a couple of hours. Others are strictly visual and just want to stare at a cock slamming into their pink blowholes. They get off on that visual.

Some like being pinned and held down where they can't go anywhere and are just fucked like a doll. They may even like being choked, slapped, spit on, spanked, their hair pulled or led around like a dog on a leash. As much as sex can be a mental experience for men, so it is for the girls. As the saying goes, "You never can know what is in the mind of a woman", so it is with these girls in front of the camera.

They've signed on for the ride so it safe to assume that they love sex. There are those who come into the industry who offer nothing on camera and these people should be cut out like a bad cancer. They are nothing but sexual pincushions and often sound like the squeaky toy their little fucking dogs chew on at home. All the rest that bring there "A game", party on!

* Many of the scenes you see today portray rough sex. The girls that perform in these scenes are always aware of what the scene will be like and many do like that aspect of sex. If they are not comfortable with rough sex, they have the

choice in not doing the scene. Before the scene is filmed, the girl will usually discuss with the actor what they are comfortable with and what they are not comfortable with doing in the scene. Nothing is forced on them. They do somewhat control the scene.

Chapter 25- Do you ever get performance anxiety?

With any type of activity where there is the element of performance, one can get a certain amount of anxiety. Actors, singers, public speakers, athletes-they all get the butterflies. The same goes for me as well. Occasionally, I would get anxious about how a scene would pan out with someone I hadn't worked with before. Sometimes the girl and I didn't seem to have a connection while we were in the green room. When I say connection, I'm referring to the exchange where two people meet and make an effort to chat and kind of get a baseline of familiarity with each other. I mean, for God sakes, we're going to fuck! At least know my favorite color, right?

The environment in which we would find ourselves filming under was always a concern as well. I remember one scene I shot for Ultimate Pictures taking place outside in the woods near Big Bear Lake in California in the winter with temperatures hovering around 40 degrees. One hundred yards away I could see the skiers lining up for the lifts. I was afraid someone would see us and call the police. It was not a comfortable environment to perform in and I was also concerned that the cold weather would hamper my ability to maintain an erection for the scene.

But there is the other extreme as well. The Wicked Pictures release Western Nights was filmed in the middle of the summer months in Arizona, where the temperature was 100 degrees in the shade! In fact, there is a threesome scene with Jonathan Morgan, Tara Hart and I outside of a stagecoach, cooking in the blazing desert sun, in which we almost had sunstroke by the end of the scene because there was no shade or tent set up for us to take breaks while filming.

Sometimes, I would get anxious if I was working with someone for the first time that I thought was too fucking beautiful to be doing porn. Despite the fact I was perceived as a good looking and confident guy, I still had thoughts that some of these beautiful girls were "out of my league" so to speak. Of course, they were getting paid to fuck anyway; it didn't matter if it was me or someone else. Savanna Samson, Julia Ann, Racquel Darrian, Christina Angel and Kayden Kross were some of these girls I would look at and think to myself, "Why the fuck are they doing porn movies? They could at least be modeling or on some millionaire's yacht in the Mediterranean!" Because they were contract girls and considered the cream of the crop in the industry, they almost always come with an ego. A healthy ego is fine; you need that to do what we do. But an unfounded huge ego based solely on ones thinking that they are "so beautiful and everyone else is a dog" kills any desire a guy may have to fuck them. Fortunately, at the time I've worked with them, they didn't seem to have that frame of reference.

I know many guys in the business have a low opinion of girls, no matter how gorgeous they appear to be, but I was always in awe of beauty. Beautiful girls were exquisite to me.

I thought they would look at me and think, "How the fuck did I get stuck working with this guy?" Of course that wasn't the case when we did finally meet on set and found we got along quite well.

That said, there have been times where a performer I didn't know refused to work with me. It's always been an awkward thing to experience especially if I have never met the person before. I remember a time when Dasha, a Vivid contract girl, was told by her husband that he didn't want her working with me. For what reason, I'll never know. But when I did finally get to work with her after she left him, oh my god, the sex was awesome!

I always try to be nice and respectful to a girl's significant other, especially if they aren't performers in the industry. Many times I just find it creepy when a guy allows his wife or girlfriend to do porn movies and get fucked by other guys. Most of the times, they're swingers. That I can understand. But if they're not, then I'm left scratching my head as to why anyone would consent to having their girl getting drilled by dudes he doesn't know. Then I think, maybe he's just living off her earnings and doesn't have any self-respect.

I never had an ego as far as my looks were concerned. I never thought of myself as either ugly or gorgeous, just normal looking. I had always been told I was handsome but I didn't really know if that was a good thing or a bad thing. I always thought it was a nice word to use when someone wasn't "oh my god gorgeous!"

I soon found out that while others may think of these women as extremely beautiful, this is not a guarantee that these girls didn't have deep insecurities. What they found attractive in someone may not always be based on looks. My self-deprecating humor always works well to ease any anxiety a girl may feel before a scene.

Chapter 26- How often do talent get tested for STD's?

Ever since I've been in the industry, all actors had to provide a negative test result for HIV every thirty days in order to work. That has since expanded to include mandatory testing for all major STDs after incidents of gonorrhea, chlamydia, syphilis and Hep C infections entered the industry and forced Cal OSHA (the California agency charged with regulating work and job safety in the state) to tell the business that they had to clean up their act and provide "safer work conditions for people involved in filming in the adult industry", whatever that meant.

The problem with the OSHA ruling is that what applies logically to 90% of the industries in California can't be mirrored in the same manner in the adult sex industry. That is the subject of a long debate, which I won't go into now.

The bottom line is, as professional sex performers, it behooves us to get tested regularly. The industry is almost a second family for some as they spend many years working in it. If one goes on a streak of fucking civilians for a time, you don't want to give someone you really like working with an infection. It costs money and more importantly it eats away at your credibility in the industry.

Listen, everyone knows we should use condoms whenever we are sexually active with someone we don't know.

The reality is we don't always use them. One can debate the stupidity of that choice for hours. But it happens.

But herpes is the secret stigma no one wants to talk about. Actually, now it seems that it's not as big of a deal as it was twenty-five years ago.

U.S. statistics state that 1 in 4 adults has herpes and, I would add, many people in the industry have it. If they didn't have it before getting into the business, they caught the virus from someone while working in the adult business. It's hard to tell if your scene partner is having an outbreak because herpes can occur internally in the vagina where it can't be seen. It can also appear as a tiny blister not easily seen on a girl's vagina or a guy's penis. He or she may think they are just sore from over work and having rash. But what adds to the "I had no idea" syndrome is that many performers do not have a resource to go to and ask. Some are embarrassed they don't know and don't want to risk being thought of as dumb, or they do not have an open and honest relationship with a regular physician. That's if they see a regular physician at all. With the astronomical costs for health insurance and the outright robbery by hospitals in excessive charges, is it any wonder they don't?

Having an STD panel test along with the HIV test is an effective way to prevent any participants from unknowingly spreading an infection in the industry or outside of it.

HPV is a recent concern for woman and especially girls in the business. It has been linked to cervical cancer in women and up till now has not been a major concern for the industry. Currently there is no test for HPV in men but women are encouraged to get regular PAP smears from their doctors.

Currently, at this writing, the industry in California has adopted a 14 day testing strategy to limit any possible STD spreading throughout the industry.

Chapter 27- Are performers scared of contracting HIV?

This is one of the most asked questions I get about the adult business. In our lifetime, we have seen the rise of AIDS and it has affected how all of us approach sexual intimacy. Along with it came a huge amount of misinformation, fear mongering and outright lies about the risk and who is susceptible to infection.

I have always been concerned about contracting HIV. It's not something I want and the inherent risk when it came to engaging in "unprotected" sex on camera was very real for me. With that said, the industry made HIV testing mandatory many years ago. The fact that they addressed it and made every reasonable effort to make sure that no one worked in the industry that was HIV positive is worthy of merit. But some have pointed to the handful of incidents where people claimed to have contracted HIV from working in front of the camera in porn as being proof that the system doesn't work. There was a major flaw in the mindset that prevailed in the business.

In a perfect world, the system only works if every person performing in adult films has protected sex with anyone outside of the business. That would protect the talent pool. But there is no way of policing what a performer does in their private life. You have to trust that they would do the right thing 100% of the time and if they didn't, they would be honest about it. But that is not the case. Additionally, the test only means that you haven't contracted an infection up until your test date. With tests nowadays, signs of exposure to HIV can be detected as recent as 10 days. If you get tested and the next night you go home with someone and have unprotected sex with someone who has an infection, there would be no way of knowing if you were infected until you tested again. In our business that's a month later. If the viral count is low it may not even come up in a test for up to 90 days, which it referred to as the incubation period.

In the meantime, you would have worked with dozens of partners, therefore putting them and all their subsequent partners at risk. Once a test came back positive, the industry would have to go back and quarantine everyone who worked with the original positive subject and their subsequent partners would also be prevented from working AND the resulting third string of partners would also be prevented from working and filming with this list of people would be discontinued until everyone who was involved had tests come back negative 30 days later. This happened on at least four different occasions since I entered the business.

It is as real a threat now as it was then and the number of people involved in films today has quadrupled. But because of the testing the industry abides by, we reduce the risk to a percentage that is far, far below the average. Sex is not a 100 % risk free activity. Just like in football, no amount of weight training, plyometrics, steroids, padding, helmets, hits that are considered legal and whatever else can prevent a career or life threatening spinal injury. Football is the business of hitting the opponent as hard as you can. The safety measures taken have greatly reduced the number of spinal injuries over the last 15 years. Now, you take a bunch of 240 lbs. guys on to a field and have them play NFL level football without the benefit of the safety precautions, you're going to see some injured or dead at the end of the game.

The same can be applied to the adult porn industry. We have precautions in place. We are professionals working to maintain a career. We're not some 21 year old girl who thinks porn is "cool" and performs in five scenes shot in some guys apartment in London before deciding she doesn't want to do it anymore because "she met someone." While that does happen, most are in it for much longer.

Now here's the final truth about HIV infection. The groups with the most risk in contracting HIV are drug users who share needles and non-white homosexual men who fuck without condoms. Period. All the data shows this. You'll hear otherwise through the media. Don't believe it. It is blood-to-blood contact with infected people that spreads the disease. Unprotected and rough anal sex is the activity that induces tears and bleeding in the rectum. So there you have it.

Many cases of men who sleep with men trying to get into straight porn have further brought the industry under attack. These are the people that have no business being in the straight adult industry. You cannot ride both sides of the fence with endangering everyone else.

In the early days, the talent took their position in the industry very seriously and did not want to jeopardize themselves, their livelihood or anyone else's for that matter. I'm not convinced that the people in front of the camera today are as serious about maintaining the professional attitude regarding what they do for a living.

It seems that they consider it a lifestyle rather than a business, and that way of thinking will only lead to a major catastrophe for the industry. On top of that, many feel that they are entitled to do what they want as long as it makes them feel good. That sense of entitlement is a major problem with today's generation of performers.

Chapter 28- Why isn't the use of condoms mandatory?

That's a good question. After the incidents of HIV infections in the business, you would think that it would be the safest way for the industry to go on making films. In fact, some in the industry have tried to make them mandatory but have been met with enormous opposition.

Vivid Video and Wicked Pictures both adopted a condom-only policy when a second HIV infection occurred and they argued that all companies should adopt the same policy. But many of the smaller companies, who didn't have the lucrative cable distribution deals that Vivid and Wicked and others had, have argued that their business would suffer because they believe the consumers, who are mainly male, wouldn't accept condoms being shown in the films and would no longer buy their movies. They believed they sold the fantasy of unbridled sex to the consumer and, in that fantasy, no man wants to be reminded that unprotected sex is risky behavior. As the adult film industry is a vocal proponent of an individual's right to choose how they live their lives, the thought is that making the use of condoms a requirement would inhibit the constitutional rights that the industry had fought for.

It is a legal mud hole in which both sides had relevant points. Some of the talent welcomed this push for condom use but, in the end, no one can get majority consensus to adopt the policy.

Some companies even relaxed their own policy to the point where their contract girls and the performers could choose to work with or without condoms, if they so desired but they had to sign a release stating that they were offered the opportunity to use a condom, refused to use it and were aware of the risks involved and, that they would not hold the company liable if they did somehow get infected by the partner in the scene.

But for many reasons, the people who choose to work only with condoms eventually are pushed aside as some new pretty face, guy or girl, is ready to work without them.

The truth is, it makes the work harder. Condoms don't feel good. Many people have latex allergies. To start and stop, having to worry about keeping a condom on for a scene is a drag. Plus, it looks like shit on the screen; a big white intrusion in a perfectly pink pussy.

Listen, if you're really into someone, emotionally and chemically, wearing a condom might not dampen your excitement. But as we are in the business of entertaining, we don't have the luxury of always having that "connection" with someone where only a brick up against the side of the head will slow us down.

Recently a county measure in Los Angeles was passed that required the use of condoms in scenes for movie productions that filed for film permits to shoot in residential locations in Los Angeles County.

It is now being challenged in court on several legal points.

Chapter 29- Is drug use prevalent in the industry?

Does the Pope shit in the Vatican?

Back when I started in the business, I would hear stories of porn sets in the 70's having bowls of cocaine, and the cast and crew helping themselves to it during the production. But then, they would get anxious, tweak out and become difficult to work with. Some would get so high; they couldn't perform their dialogue or get an erection. I've seen girls lock themselves in a bathroom for 10 minutes while they smoked speed or coke and then, come out so whacked out of their minds, they needed to down shots of whisky or tequila so they could calm down enough to perform their scenes.

Now, if you're asking if producers provide drugs on set, the answer is no. Not the responsible ones at least. There are some producers who have come and gone that did provide drugs to select people on set--mainly the actresses. They were trying to get laid.

Marijuana is probably the most used drug in the business. Now that medical marijuana is legal in California, anyone can now march into a MM store and buy the best grade pot ever grown. They don't even hide it anymore. On set, they compare blends like they compare smartphone features.

Cocaine, meth, prescription pills, GHB and ecstasy use has also been a problem.

Hard core drug use is officially discouraged and frowned upon, but many look the other way when it is around. If a show gets done on time, then all is well. But if it impedes in finishing a show or someone performing their job, then they develop a bad reputation and few producers will hire them.

So, yes, there are drugs used by people in the business but probably no more or less than any other industry. I have had my own issues with drugs but I've worked on not letting them be a negative influence in my life anymore. I think occasional fun is okay and doing so in a responsible way. The key is to not let it take over and ruin your life. I've seen many destroyed by addiction. Even alcohol abuse has brought many careers to a dead halt.

I wouldn't say being in the industry makes someone become a drug user. I'm sure it sometimes has been introduced to someone who never came across it but since teenagers have been known to try these drugs at an early age, I doubt these new performers are angels. But the feelings of loneliness and despair that some people experience get amplified when working in the industry and drugs numb those emotions-for a short time, at least.

Chapter 30- Do you receive residual payments from your movies?

The adult film industry is not represented nor protected by the Hollywood based film and TV unions, so the pay structure is based solely on paying one time for a performance. That performance can be shown as many times as possible forever and one wouldn't receive any further money from it. The term found in model releases is "in perpetuity".

It is not normal for the industry to pay royalties on movie titles unless you are someone with a very big name and draw, someone like Tera Patrick, Jenna Jameson and Janine. Even with a name, it may not be enough leverage to negotiate a royalty deal with adult companies in today's market.

If a girl wants to make more money, she has the opportunity to go on the dance club circuit in the United States and earn good money headlining, signing photos and hosting special nights at large clubs in major cities. Many sex novelty companies pay certain performers for making molds of their pussy and asshole for latex toys. Guys with huge wangs make molds of their cocks to be marketed as dildos. They receive an initial payment with subsequent monthly payments totaling 24 months usually.

A girl can host her own personal website where she can offer customized videos for her fans and selling personalized merchandise. She can also work in the high priced escort business and make quite a lot of money sleeping with paying clients.

This is why you never hear of a millionaire porn star. A millionaire has a net worth of over one million dollars in investments excluding the equity in their home or alimony; or they need to have an annual income of one million or more per year.

There are no millionaire porn stars. Maybe Jenna Jameson was a millionaire because she and her ex-husband sold CLUBJENNA.COM for a reported high eight-figure amount. He also owned a majority share of the company so she may have walked away a six-figure amount after their divorce.

She recently came back to do cam shows after quite famously declaring she would "never spread her legs again for the industry".

Chapter 31- Do the girls fake their orgasms?

I believe that many of the actresses enjoy the sex they have on screen, whether it's with men or women. And given the fact that some get to choose who they work with on screen, it makes it easier for them to enjoy the sex and get off on screen. There are some who get so turned on during their scenes, they don't even think about their performance. They just want to have as many orgasms as possible.

There are different reasons for their hyper-sexuality. Some love the attention they receive on set, some thrive on the idea of thousands of viewers watching and masturbating to their scenes, and some block out of their minds the fact they are working on a film set and just connect with the other actor. Others get off on being treated and fucked like an object. They love the humiliation factor and this is what gets them off. Some think they are the center of the universe and that everyone on the planet wants them.

There are some, however, who can't achieve real orgasms on film. They're either disconnected from the other actor or they need some other stimulation--mental, physical or pharmaceutical--in order to let themselves go while performing in front of the camera. Occasionally, anal penetration, clitoral stimulation, or a vibrator is needed for them to cum.

Still, others do not want to orgasm on screen because they are "in a relationship with someone" and feel that having a real climax is something that they should share only with their significant other. That is the stupidest thing I've ever heard. That is akin to playing professional baseball and hoping to strike out at every plate appearance.

At times though, you can tell that they are going through the motions. When the director is ready for their big 'O' and they are not at that point in real time, they will count to ten and let out a big loud fake orgasm for the benefit of the viewers.

Chapter 32- Aren't the girls victims of molestation?

Sadly, this is very often the case. And not just in regards to the woman, but sometimes the men as well. Whether it was a onetime occurrence or a systematic series of encounters with someone in their family, a close friend, an authority figure in the community, these episodes have deeply affected some of the people in the adult film industry.

What's interesting is that these events often happen among families in very conservative religious organizations and communities. Mormons, Jehovah's Witnesses, Church of the Latter Day Saints, the Catholic Church and other smaller, lesser known sects have all had enormous amounts of these incidents being reported that involved their "God fearing" and "Christian" members.

This isn't an attack on these groups. I find it ironic that the same people who subscribe to a doctrine of abstinence before marriage, believe that masturbation is a sin, and the natural curiosity and exploration of one's own sexuality is a dirty thing, seem to have a higher percentage of people who engage in depraved sexual acts with underage children, thus scarring them for life and making them prone to get involved with the sex industry in some aspect.

I am not an expert on this subject nor do I pretend to have some special insight. All I can speak from is my experience of what I observed and what was related to me by others in the business.

Though never sexually abused as a child, I was exposed to nudity and the woman's naked form because I happened to have gorgeous baby sitters who all seemed comfortable being topless or naked around me as a boy growing up. I remember admiring one babysitter's ass at the age of four. She would wash dishes in the kitchen in her white panties and catch me stealing looks at her while hiding behind a doorframe in the living room. Never once did she attempt to cover up or put pants on. She probably thought the curiosity of a boy was a natural and harmless expression.

It was these instances that awakened my desire for women when I was a boy, and that could have very well been an influence on me when I decided to go into the adult industry. But as a child, I was taught by my mother's church that it was improper to have desires or sexual thoughts relating to the opposite sex.

Repression eventually leads to expression, and not always in a healthy way.

Chapter 33- Would you work with someone you didn't like personally?

There have been times when a potential scene partner has irritated the fuck out of me. Whether it was that fact they talked non-stop during the scene or the pitch in their voice, it made it hard for me to get into the scene.

I am lucky in the fact that, more often than not, I am given my choice of who I want to work with. But sometimes, after the initial scene, I will decide I do not want to work with them again because I really don't like them. I'd rather work with someone I like than do a scene where there is no passion.

I don't like it when girls aren't present, especially emotionally. If the scene is just a stand-alone scene, it doesn't really matter. But if it's a scene in a story driven feature, I need to know they are at least trying their best. It makes it difficult to connect and connection is a key part of what I need in order to do the best scene possible. No one wants the scene to turn into some gymnastic workout where there is lots of action but no real substance.

There are times when the girls are more worried about their fucking hair looking beautiful on camera than being real and engaging in a scene. Again, I think that viewers prefer to see someone engaged and present in what they are doing on screen, not someone going through the motions.

When you watch guys like Rocco Siffredi and Manuel Ferrara fuck girls, you see how "into" the girls they are. They're looking deep into the girl's eyes and making them really respond to being fucked.

Guys don't like being the only one to do all the work. They don't want to be forced to carry the scene. It happens more often than you would think and that is why a good male performer who can overcome that and still finish and make a scene look exciting is hard to come by today. You can see the frustration on the faces of the guys as they try and perform a great scene.

The most uncomfortable situation you can find yourself in is when you are booked with someone and you look at their photos and they look awesome. Then, when you finally arrive on set, you think to yourself, "What happened to the hot chick I saw in the photos?" This happens quite a bit. The performers are usually only booked by their photos on some agency web site. That's when you find out that the agents haven't updated the pictures in six months to reflect how the talent looks presently and then it creates a tense situation for the director and the talent. The girl has been chomping on mashed potatoes and beer while she gets over some douchebag she was dating and in the meantime gains 16 lbs. The actor doesn't want to fuck the girl and the director doesn't want to send the girl home. The same situation with the men happens as well. Guys are working a lot and let themselves go mainly because they're to tired to hit the gym after a long day on set.

If a director is committed to shooting the best possible product, he will send her home and find a replacement. No one wants to be the "bad guy", but it leaves the actor in a place where it makes his job more awkward.

Then of course, the higher ups in a company may send a memo down to production to abstain from hiring certain people until they shape up.

Listen, this business is about sex and the players have to look the part. We are selling the fantasy. You have to look good in this business. If a runway or print model shows up to a "go-see" and she is overweight, she is sent away and not booked until she has lost the weight, simple as that. No one has any qualms saying what it is. But in the adult business, everyone is so afraid of making someone upset that they don't do or say anything. They settle for mediocrity.

It's up to the actor to decide if he can and will perform with this girl and that is a hard decision for him. The best thing that can be done is for the director and the company to stand their ground and refuse to hire someone who hasn't maintained the shape that they had when the photos were used to book them. It is the agency's responsibility to make sure their site's pictures are current and the models maintain the shape and look that the companies rely on when booking talent for video productions because high definition video is unforgiving.

Chapter 34- Do you date the girls you work with in front of the camera?

I have "dated" some of the girls I've worked with; some briefly and others for longer periods of time. Sometimes, we head out to a bar or a restaurant for food and drinks and then head off to my place or hers for sex. Maybe we catch a movie. Sometimes, it was just a page or a text or a phone call to "come on over and hang out". Other times, it is maybe for a night or a week of casual togetherness in a hotel room.

When I first got into the business, I had no interest in having a steady monogamous relationship. Not to say that if I did happen to come across someone that I liked, someone who was fun and engaging, that I wouldn't ask them out. But I kept my feelings at a distance and was satisfied to keep it casual.

I had some issues at the time as far as what was acceptable to me in regards to a relationship with another performer and one of the things I couldn't get past was the fact that if I really liked a girl, I wouldn't want her having sex with other guys in front of the camera.

My fear was she would maybe develop feelings for another guy, much like she may have developed for me, and she would eventually lose interest and drop me for the new guy.

I feared this because I knew what a short attention span we performers in the industry operate with. When you're young, you are easily distracted and prone to stupid rash decisions. The people in the business aren't known for having focus, determination and sticking things out when relationships become difficult. They just move on to the next best thing.

To be fair, I had done the same thing in my life repeatedly. I realized what was going to be the pattern in these mini-relationships. Mostly, I would designate the encounters as a strictly physical attraction between two horny people who got along on set and amused each other. But I knew that, if I let myself believe that I was falling in love with someone, the reality was that I was just smitten with good sex.

Chapter 35- Is it true that some guys in the industry started in gay porn?

There were a few guys that had started in gay porn and through some luck were able to crossover into straight porn films. Jeff Stryker, Peter North, Mark Wallace, and Eric Price were guys who made the jump to straight porn.

But most of the other guys were strippers or boyfriends of girls in the industry. In later years, there were some who had performed solo masturbation scenes geared towards the gay market. That wasn't held against them as much as someone who actually had sex with men.

There were some girls who would turn down working with a guy because they had done gay scenes at one time or were rumored to be bisexual in the private lives. Recently in the last few years, there have been male performers in straight porn who have moved over to gay porn. Recently, Rocco Reed was the latest high profile straight performer who has crossed over to do gay porn. Why he did it, only he knows. I guess he was always bi-sexual and preferred to fuck men instead of women.

I never had a problem with these guys as long as they didn't ride both sides of the fence at the same time. Peter North, who had the most celebrated career and was quite well known by his stage name from the gay movie genre, was always a cool guy and we had a great time hanging out on set. But he was done with the gay movies and never did them again when he started working in straight porn.

There are guys working in gay films who claim to be "gay for pay" and swear that they are straight in their personal lives. Many have girlfriends or wives. But since the pay for these guys is not exceedingly much more than what straight guys in straight porn get paid, I wonder if they are just bi-sexual but refuse to acknowledge it.

Chapter 36- Does double penetration feel strange to you?

Seeing a woman take two men inside her- one in her ass and one in her pussy- I feel is one of the more arousing things a man can see. Totally giving up her orifices to be filled with cock is as much of a mental turn on as it is physical. I've performed DP's on girls in the industry and for the most part enjoyed doing the scenes. If you watch a lot of porn from Europe, this seems to be the usual kind of sex scene. It's almost seems mandatory if a girl wants to have any length of career in the porn shot in Europe.

But for a lot of men the thought of having another man's penis so close to theirs scares them. To be honest, when you are inside a woman you see another guy's mug in your peripheral vision and feel his joint rubbing up against yours, yeah, it is a bit uncomfortable. Guys get freaked out because they think enjoying a woman's pussy or ass when you feel another man's cock practically next to yours, somehow makes you gay. It doesn't. Not that there's anything wrong with being gay.

Double penetration does make the woman feel tighter and seeing her react to the heightened level of sensation can be arousing. But focusing on the girl's reaction is the only arousing thing about it and, frankly, DP was my least favorite scene to do in the business. Love to watch it, hate doing it.

Chapter 37- Do the girls really enjoy anal sex?

There are many girls in the industry who love anal sex and practice it in their personal lives. And there are some who don't enjoy it but will do it as they get paid more money when they agree to perform an anal sex scene. As a performer, I can usually tell when a girl is really enjoying it or doing it just for the money. If they aren't, you usually see a pained look on their face as they try and endure however many minutes it takes to do the scene. It is amazing what a girl will go through for that little extra dough.

And the same goes for the guys too. Some guys don't like doing anal sex scenes with girls on camera and there are some who only want to do anal scenes with girls. "Straight to anal" they call it. No vaginal penetration allowed. When I was a new performer, I didn't have that much experience with anal sex so it was a little strange and a little off-putting. But they also paid guys more money to do anal scenes and so, like many other guys, agreed to do it for the larger rate. After a while, I began to really enjoy doing it and, even when they stopped paying the extra money, I would always inquire, "Is it an anal scene?"

Sometimes, the girl and I will be so into our scene, that I may mention how much I would love to fuck their ass and they let me slide my cock inside their asshole. Of course, it happens when the camera isn't filming so as to not give the producer a free anal scene.

I have even seen girls turn to the director and say "I want to get fucked in the ass, you got the money in the budget?" If he has it, then away we go. If not, then that's it, no anal...at least on camera!

Chapter 38- What do you do if a girl has bad hygiene?

Usually, most everyone who works in the industry makes a concerted effort to be clean and take proper care of themselves when filming. In the cases where a girl may not be so fresh "down there", I always try to avoid a potentially embarrassing moment with them and make a joke like "Okay, all the vegetables are washed and ready to be eaten, right?" or something along those lines.

Another trick, when in doubt, is to do a finger check- sneakily putting a finger inside her as part of the foreplay and then taking a sniff when the camera is focused on another part of her body. I've known some girls to have a perpetual sour smell down there because they were secret drinkers at home-- pounding bottles of wine instead of water. That can lead to a tainted taste as their pH level is affected.

In the end, most girls are very clean as they take showers and douche before and after a scene. Though, there have been times when a girl has left a sponge in the vagina and forgot about it for a day or two. That always creates a big stink.

One time, working with a girl I'll just refer to as J.H., she smelled so bad that I had to breathe through my mouth instead of my nose so that I could get through the scene. After the scene, I ran to the bathroom to wash myself with iodine. Thankfully, she didn't have anything disease wise but she stank like a dirty dishrag.

Chapter 39- Why do they give out acting awards for porn movies?

Acting awards for porn movies has always been a source of a good laugh for the general public. Seeing a girl onstage, crying because she won an award for anal starlet of the year is surreal. An actor thanking their mother for her support of their career gets a few eye rolls as well.

Yes, it's true some of the worst acting can be seen in adult films because most of the talents performing in front of the camera are not trained as actors. While some are comfortable in front of the camera and can recite their lines, it is another thing to actually be able to give a character on paper in a poorly written script some dimension and depth. And to be fair, there are plenty of actors and actresses on TV and in films who can be just as bad themselves.

Keep in mind these scripts contain five or six sex scenes, so the emphasis isn't on developing a thorough story arc or character arc as it may be in traditional screenplays.

If an adult film is 80 minutes and each sex scene runs about 12 to 17 minutes length, you can see that the rest of the film is filler. They just want to get from point A to point C as easily as they can.

There have been many who have tried their best to do a great job and make their roles believable. I am one of those people. And it's always nice to be recognized for one's effort. As some films had budgets that allowed for rehearsal time, we worked to flesh out the material and tweak the dialogue into something that was much more believable. There are many directors who actually care about making the best movie they can with the limited budgets they have. They sometimes use that experience in adult films to better their craft as filmmakers and some move on to work in mainstream films or TV. But if you asked them, many would never admit to having first learned their chops from shooting porn.

Even if it sounds corny, we still like to dress up for one night a year and have our work acknowledged. We pretend that we are at a real award show like the ones we've watched growing up such as the Oscars or the Golden Globes. For us, it's our one night for glamour and fun.

Chapter 40- How many awards have you won?

In the time I've been in the industry, I have seen award shows come and go. From small regional shows to the large ones in Las Vegas that are attended by the industry's biggest stars as well as company people. The big one for a long time was the AVN Awards. These were referred to as the "Oscars of Porn" for a number of years by the mainstream media. It was the one event that everyone looked forward to attending, winning or at least getting fucked up beyond recognition without it hurting their reputation.

Since then, the XBIZ Awards have also become the highlighted award event of the year, along with the XRCO (*) Awards bringing up the rear. I've even had the privilege of hosting the AVN Awards. It is a fun evening where we get to dress up and act like we are just like the stars we see on TV.

I have had the honor of being recognized for my contribution to adult films with 11 AVN trophies, 2 Hall of Fame Awards from AVN and XRCO, 2 XBIZ Awards and 4 XRCO Awards.

*XRCO- X Rated Critics Organization

Chapter 41- Do the awards have any meaning for you?

Every year around the time the AVN nominations were announced, I would get a knot in my stomach. This was where I was going to see if the performances I felt were my best would be noticed.

"Performances?" you say? Well, I know it's a little much to keep from laughing. But as long as there are people in the industry just going through the motions and showing up to fuck, there are still others that actually try to do the best they can on all fronts. Whether it's a role that requires them to embody a character or just performing a sexy hot scene for the viewer, there are those who aspire to be a much more in the industry than a hole or a cock.

As long as there is room to do something more with a role, I try my best. Whether it's comedic or dramatic, I've tried to entertain. Yes, I have studied improvisational comedy and have also done scene study work with various coaches in Hollywood. It all helps to make me a better performer.

I'm a fan of good films and I always dissect performances to see what critical points in the story the actor hit properly to make his portrayal believable. Then I steal from them.

Having read many books on the art of story writing, cinematography and how to break down and flesh out a character's back story, I have slowly been able to better equip myself to bring something to the screen. Whether or not I get the opportunity to do that in these types of films is another thing all together.

Most of the time, we don't have time to shoot take after take to get it right. As an example, the bathroom scene (Help me help you!) in Jerry Maguire between Tom Cruise and Cuba Gooding Jr. took three days to shoot. One scene in three days! Do you realize how many takes of film were shot over the course of three days? If we had that time, we could probably do just as well. (Probably not!)

But we don't and that is one of the reasons why porn is the quality it is today.

Chapter 42- Will a porn actress have sex with me off-camera?

Possibly. Many are willing to work as escorts or "companions" as they can charge far more money for far fewer hours of "work". If you do happen to meet one of these girls, don't assume that she is doing that. If your intention is to sleep with one of these girls and you are willing to pay for it, you may want to be discreet in how you broach the subject. It could lead to an embarrassing and awkward situation for you both. You don't want to approach them with the attitude that they are some whore who will fuck anybody for money.

Let them bring it up if that's what you're interested in but discuss it elegantly. In the end, be smart and safe about that whole subject.

I know personally that a lot of these girls go to New York and escort for certain agencies that specialize in delivering porn stars for the discriminating client. A lot of these clients are Wall Street cowboys who make huge amounts of money "robbing" people of their hard earned money in the markets. They work such a high stress job that they party hard on their off hours. You can't blame them though as most will be dead of a heart attack by the time they're 50. Live and let live. A girl has got to eat too!

Chapter 43- Are people allowed to visit the porn set?

As popular as adult films have been with the consumers, we have always had some sort of press or media on the set for a day to write and report on the feature for the industry magazines in order to promote the titles to distributors and store owners. This is the same reason you see mainstream magazines chock full of interviews coming from the sets of big Hollywood films and network television shows. It promotes the show, so the studios can charge more money by selling the broadcast rights and advertising time for a successful show.

And yes, we would invite a friend or a celebrity that we may have met to come and hang out on set. I've invited many of the celebrities I came into contact with in Hollywood to come and see for themselves what it was actually like to be on a adult film set.

What was interesting for many of these actors was that they saw how difficult it was to perform dialogue without much rehearsal time.

Many of them told me that there would be no way that they could even attempt to act without some time being spent going over with the director what they thought about the character, the scene, and all that other actor shit they talk about.

They take their craft seriously and couldn't imagine allowing themselves to be filmed without a good amount of rehearsal or even a decent script. Which, when you think about, goes against the craft where they teach you that one needs to forget ones vanity in order to completely immerse oneself in a role. But that is totally different from being prepared. A good actor wants to be prepared by knowing his character inside and out.

They also get a sense of the camaraderie we have on set and how comfortable we are with our own nakedness and sexuality in general. Seeing a naked male actor with his semi erect penis chatting to the grip about some highlights from a football game is not something you would expect to see everyday. Hearing a girl offhandedly talk about her hygiene routine as 'getting the sand out of her clam' can be shocking to the first time observer. But their overall impression is that they hadn't realized how professional and businesslike it is working on a porn set. They realized that the quality of the final product had more to do with the lack of time and money as opposed to just talent and skill.

Chapter 44- Since you have sex for a living, how do you view sex in your personal life?

For me, sex has always been more about the romance than the physical dominance of one over the other. That's what you see on the screen in many porn movies. I don't necessarily like to have "Olympic games" sex. I'd much rather take my time to relate to a girl and discover her nuances - because that's what turns me on. Finding their ticklish spot, seeing if they enjoy having their toes sucked or discovering how they react to a new sensation is always fun. I obviously found something attractive about her in the first place, so I want to find out what else

I like about her that may not be so apparent. I've noticed after some years that my view on sex hasn't really strayed far from what I liked when I was younger.

For instance, bondage sex was never something I watched or enjoyed participating in. But as time progressed, I found myself drawn towards it. I went as far as to engage in certain types of BDSM with partners in my personal life. But after a being away from the business at one point, I found myself returning to the way I originally approached sex, which was with excitement and a genuine interest in connecting with a girl.

I craved the kind of intimacy in which the world stops and all you can feel is the breathing of the other person and the throbbing of their pussy; that level of connection where you want to blurt out, "I love you!" because the pleasure is so overpowering, even when you know it's a passing moment triggered by the flood of endorphins to your brain.

Not only am I much more particular about who I pursue an encounter with, I also take time to observe how that person acts around others and from that, I decide whether or not they are even worth my continued interest. Not because I think I'm better than them, but because at this point in my life, I know exactly what I want in a person - and I know what I won't put up with. If being with them doesn't enhance my experience of life in some way, I'm totally okay with not doing a thing with them.

Chapter 45- Do the actresses work as prostitutes?

Some do. Many have tried prostitution to some extent prior to performing in adult films. There was a time when being an adult film actress was the pinnacle for a woman unabashedly in charge of her own sexuality. Some had come from that world of prostitution mainly because they wanted to view themselves as legitimate objects of desire as opposed to feeling anonymous.

Now, it seems that with the focus these days being about money and shopping and a bling-bling lifestyle, it's not a surprise that the girls go to Las Vegas, New York, London and the Arab countries in order to work as prostitutes. To be quite honest, very few of the girls in the industry now could survive in the world of high-priced escorts. The girls in that world are usually the most beautiful girls in the world. From what I know, if you are blessed with being extremely beautiful, you can earn much more money than you would earn on a film set.

But with so many beautiful girls having worked in real modeling and runway shows making themselves available for escorting, many of the girls in the industry can't compete with them. These girls are exotic looking, educated and often speak several languages. Compare that to most American girls and it's no contest as to who may get more money.

In fact, I had dated one well-known porn star for close to a year when she decided to go to

New York for ten days - and came back with over $30k in money earned from escorting. And that was after she paid the agency's forty percent cut for booking the clients.

I've known for years certain girls who did engage in prostitution. And I've also known that certain company owners would introduce girls to other business "associates" with the unspoken understanding that these girls may provide sexual favors for some sort of financial compensation.

Is there a difference between being an adult film actress or a high-end call girl? It depends on the story one tells oneself. Should they be judged according to what they do? I don't think that is fair. Like the good book says, "Let he who is without sin, cast the first stone."

Chapter 46- Are the performers in adult films swingers?

The swinging lifestyle is something that has been kept under wraps for many years. From working-class couples, to the upper echelons of the powerful and elite, swinging or "wife swapping" has been practiced, until recently, behind closed doors. Many who did engage secretly in swinging and wife swapping did so under the constant fear of being found out.

Given the fact that this country was, for the most part, founded by people who espoused puritanical religious beliefs, many feared that they could lose their jobs, their homes, their children and be ostracized from their communities. Add to that, the antiquated local laws that penalized any sexual activity deemed "unnatural, devious, perverted and a sin against God and church" and criminal punishment for sexual relations outside the marriage, it easy to understand that this was a serious concern for many.

When "free love" was championed in the 1960's as a way of genuinely expressing love for all people, some took that to include sex with anyone they wanted or desired, whether married or single. The premise of swinging, as explained by many, was to allow each partner the chance to exercise their primal urges and not have to resist what was a natural desire for one or many potential sexual partners. To be constrained by commonly accepted forms of social and moral behavior aggravates them. They want to do what they want and with whom they want. Obviously, people who gravitated towards this swinging lifestyle and who were attractive looking and open to the idea of sexual display for the enjoyment of others found themselves curious about what the porn industry could offer them in terms of an attractive outlet for their way of life. Good money, recognition among fans, and a constant supply of new and exciting partners made entering the adult film business the perfect solution for people who were swingers.

Now, swinging seems to be more of a pastime with the latest generation of performers in the business. Some are oversexed, while others are seeking out new sexual encounters to replace a growing feeling of complacency or boredom in their own lives.

Others feel they should have sex at every opportunity that presents itself-because they are a porn performer and believe they have to be "on display" all the time. And there are still those who seek a more genuine, deeper connection.

There are those in relationships with other talent who participate in swinger meet-ups, either with industry peers or people not in the industry. I participated in some of these parties, attending with new girls who just came into the business. They were curious and wanted to see what these parties were like. If the situation presented itself and they found someone they liked, they trusted that I would look out for their safety.

The surprising fact is that many performers - female and male - actually have very limited sex outside of the industry. They are either dating someone and only have sex with others through work on set, or they don't have personal sex at all, as is the case of a girl who works 3 to 6 times a week and needs time for her ass or vagina to heal.

Chapter 47- What level of education do the performers possess?

Many people make the assumption that individuals who end up in the adult film business are uneducated and lack a sense of direction in their lives. They wouldn't be 100% wrong.

There are some who have made their way into the business without finishing high school or attending college. But, I have found is that most people in the industry have at least finished their high school education. Granted, some may not be able to name the 50 state capitals in the U.S. or speak about the implications of

Keynesian economics in the 21st century, but they are not as uneducated as one would imagine.

There are a few who attend college while working in the industry but keep it a secret, as they do not want to be hounded and bothered by students who may be fans of their work and happen to attend the same university.

But at the same time it's very hard to resist the money offered to them to work on days that they may be in class. Productions don't work around a girl performer's schedule and if she feels she maybe losing more money than she's trying to earn while in school, some end up dropping out of the semester, thinking they will return after they are done for whatever length of time they think they will get the most work.

The problem is once you enter into this line of work, you have little motivation to expand your mind and stretch your mental prowess in a different direction. That has to come from a personal desire to want to excel in life. You can find yourself becoming dumbed down to a certain extent because the business may consume a large amount of your attention and time. The people you end up spending the bulk of your time with are usually people who don't have a direction or a goal in their life. They go from day-to-day, month-to-month with no real plan as to what they want to do after porn.

*ROI- return on investment

Chapter 48- How hard is it to have a relationship with someone who is not is the adult industry?

As most people find out it life, can be very hard to maintain a relationship with someone who doesn't share the same values as you.

When you are in the sex business, you are using sex as a means to attain the quality of life you want, and obviously sex and love are two separate entities. That paradigm of thinking bothers many people because they want to feel that the sex act should be based solely on love. Because of this notion, we can't tell when someone is being truthful or just going through the motions with us; we confuse sex and love as being the same thing. We have forever been ingrained with the idea that the lust and sexual attraction one feels for another human being is a bad thing and the byproduct of someone who has a no self-control over their mind.

Some have been raised to believe that if you can't control your thoughts and desires, you are a bad person. On the flip side of the coin, all we do as humans, for the most part, is try to attract people to us by our clothing, behavior, accomplishments and words. Whether for business, social, or other reasons, that is in our animal DNA. We cannot ignore our biological and social urges. We are all tribal in certain respects. How one fails to address these instincts is usually what creates problems in relationships.

Secondly, because adult film performers are so physical in expressing love and lust, someone in a relationship with them may be concerned that their partner may find someone else more attractive than them. Maybe they have bigger tits, a firmer ass, a thicker cock, a leaner body- whatever physical attribute that draws their attention in the first place- and that insecurity can cause a rift in the relationship.

We are all insecure as it is, and we have this belief that when we pair up with someone, we become the "end all and be all" for the other person's sexual needs and desires. We believe that they will never find another person as attractive as us and they wouldn't even imagine what it would be like to be intimate with another person. This way of thinking is what makes it difficult for many to have relationships with present and former adult performers.

There are sources that delve into this subject who can eloquently speak about why the "slut factor" plays a pivotal role in mate selection.

* Slut factor- the common theory that a man wants a slut in the bedroom but a lady in dining room. For woman, a bad boy in bed but a gentleman all other times.

Chapter 49- With hardcore porn so prevalent, why are softcore sex films still being produced?

There is a segment of the viewing public who still enjoy watching the fantasy of "forbidden sex" played out on the screen. The anticipation of sex is still the strongest aphrodisiac among people and some would prefer to see sex portrayed as an act of mutual attraction between people as opposed to the domination of a man over a woman.

Women may fantasize about being dominated in sex but they don't always want to view that type of sex on screen. They will tell you that what gets them excited and turned on are the feelings or memories they experience when they are with someone. That initial attraction, feeling safe with someone, and that person being slow and sensual in their discovery of the other person's body is what excites them. That is their version of a "spank bank."

The soft-core films today are shot with a romantic tone to the love scenes, as opposed to sex being portrayed as a cardio class like it is in many hardcore porn films. This allows for more exposition and emotional plot points to be played out in the softcore movie.

As widely available as TV channels are that show hardcore sex today, there are also channels worldwide that want sexy, provocative content without the stigma of hardcore pornography attached to it. Softcore films entice the viewers, but give the broadcasters some protection against possibly losing advertising dollars and premium subscribers if they are considered purveyors of hardcore pornography.

*Soft-core porn by definition is an adult movie whereby penetration is not actually shown and women's genitalia is often shot where you only see the pubic hair but not the vaginal opening. A man's cock is usually not shown erect, if shown at all. These are the "rules" here in the United States for broadcast on certain channels where access is unrestricted to minors. Elsewhere, especially in Europe, the "rules" are a little more liberal. Some argue this has happened because of the excessive feminism in the last generation that seeks to disempower men and eradicate any display of the phallic symbol in today's media.

Chapter 50- How do you feel about being recognized by people because of your films?

Being recognized from porn can be a two edged sword. There has always been a need in some people for significance; to be famous or known to a larger group of people other than their immediate circle of friends and family. But there is also an inherent need for anonymity; where we can just be ourselves without feeling that we are always being watched or on display.

When I first started out, it was a stroke to my ego to be recognized. Then, when people would actually remember my name that became an even bigger ego stroke for me. The fact that someone would remember my name was cool to me. I have never had an awkward encounter when approached by a fan or from being recognized in public. Everyone has been cordial and displayed an amount of tactfulness.

But there are times when I feel I can't relax because someone is watching me because they have recognized me from their porn collection.

I have to watch what I say, my behavior and how I carry myself as I don't want it to disappoint or do something that will later end up in someone's tale of a embarrassing incident.

Nowadays, I don't concern myself with it as much. I've always tried to conduct myself with grace and class (except on Tequila Tuesdays). It's nice to know that I may have had an impact on a person's life in some small way, so much so that they remember my face and name. But it was never my goal just to be famous or to be recognized by millions of people. I especially value anonymity now in the wake of social media being the outlet for many people desperate to be famous and willing to do anything to attain it.

Chapter 51- Do male fans want you to have sex with their wives or girlfriends?

There have been occasions where guys who were fans approached me and mentioned their desire to see their girlfriend or wife engage sexually with one of their favorite male porn stars.

That is something I can't really wrap my head around.

I'm flattered that someone would entrust me to be a safe and respecting sex partner for his significant other – but that isn't my bag.

However, I do know of many male performers who do this sort of thing. Some advertise and do it for money and some do it because that's what they think they are supposed to be to people- just a penis. They think they always have to perform and prove themselves sexually.

Chapter 52- Would you allow your kids to go into the adult business?

I have no children, but I like to think that I would be a parent who would respect the choices my children would make when they became adults. With that said, I would be severely disappointed if they chose to make a career in adult films. Of course, by the time they would be grown and old enough to make that decision, there may not be any porn industry left in California!

It's my experience that, despite whether it's right or wrong to hold someone's adult film work against them, the reality is that it can severely limit your opportunities in leading a successful, fulfilling life after the porn industry. It's just the way it is. There may be an occasional black swan event, but it is rare.

People love to hold shit over other people's heads and the fact that one may have been in the porn industry only adds to that. I can think of dozens of incidents where someone who had moved on and was working a regular job, be it as a nurse, teacher or otherwise, have been outed and fired from their jobs. For something they did years ago!

Chapter 53- Why are people losing their jobs after it's discovered they have performed in adult films?

Moral clauses are being written into all types of employment contracts these days. Many corporations and businesses have extended their reach to include the argument that their employee's images and personal reputation are, by association, extensions of the corporate brand. Past indiscretions or questionable moral behavior can be looked at as a liability in today's competitive marketplace, where any negative exposure in one's personal life can be seen as a negative reflection on the brand itself. You've heard of people being fired for shit they posted on their Facebook accounts? There you go.

If an employee of a company has a video of them engaging in a sex film that is readily viewable on the internet and, while meeting with clients or potential clients, this comes to light, it can mean lost revenue for that company and may potentially damage the company's reputation. They wouldn't be taken seriously, regardless of their current position.

Most people in the corporate workplace are conservative by association (though the shit they do in their off time in Thailand would make the Devil blush) and most would look at a porn past as a questionable moral choice.

Because of this, companies would choose to keep an employee with less risk of harming their image than someone who has the potential to embarrass the brand. This is a fact that most of us didn't consider when we decided to go into adult films. We didn't think it through in terms of what would be an acceptable background for a potential employer.

What you chose to do in your past can have ramifications for years to come and seriously impede the chances of moving on to another career and making a good living once you've left the adult film business.

Chapter 54- Do you feel the industry has empowered the woman as some have claimed?

That really depends on your definition of empowerment. But I will say this; there is no skill-set that one can learn from being in the adult business that cannot be learned somewhere else; not even blowjobs.

One could argue they are empowered if they would take advantage of the flexible schedule the business provides them to go to university, get a degree in a field that allows them to move on to better paying careers where advancement and longevity are more likely than the short shelf life the adult film industry has.

Many girls eventually go on and start a new life as a wife or mother, and put the business behind them. Even some directors and production crew will go on to work on TV shows and films, or move toward developing web and photography sites.

Still, some others will choose to make themselves the victim and tell anyone who will listen how bad they had it in the business. I think if anyone is empowered, it is by being reflective, honest and own up to the mistakes they may have made and moving ahead with their decision to make better choices for the future.

Chapter 55- How does a performer choose their stage name?

There has always been a joke that to find your porn name, you take the name of your first pet and the name of the first street you remember growing up on and that would become your porn stage name.

Mine would have been Thor Woodstock; not very sexy- rugged but not sexy.

But in earlier days, agents usually picked the names for the girls and no one actually knows what their guidelines were. Sometimes a girl would resemble someone famous and they give herself the same name but with a variation on the spelling. Or some will take a name and twist it into some sexual play on words like Arnold Schwarzenpecker, Fanny O'Rear or Mike Hunt.

Whatever method was used, the intent was to give that person some anonymity so that they wouldn't have the police raiding their homes and arresting them.

Up until 1987, the filming of porn movies in Los Angeles County was illegal and some sets were raided and shut down. You could be held for 24 hours in jail and charged with indecent exposure.

The government has always been suspected of keeping a list of people's names that were in the adult film industry, so that if at some point they wanted to prosecute the video companies on charges of obscenity, they could also charge the actors and actresses as willing accomplices. Having a pseudonym was a way to protect oneself.

I chose my stage name from my uncle who had used it while he worked as an undercover drug agent for a federal agency. I thought it was different enough without sounding "porn-like" and that it would not be easily confused with someone else's name.

Chapter 56- Do you watch porn films?

It would seem crazy that someone, who has had as much sex as I have had in my personal life as well as adult films, would even want to watch more porn- but I do.

I prefer European porn to American porn. I know many of the girls in American porn and, though there are some who are my favorites, I'm not really interested in watching them narrate sex scenes with "Yeah, you like fucking my little pussy, don't you? Huh? Yeah, you're dirty! Yeah, oh my god! Yeah, I'm a whore, etc, etc". (Of course now, there are way too many new girls in porn movies and I don't know who's who anymore.)

Also, I think the European girls are more naturally feminine. They have less plastic surgery, they are naturally slender and fit, and they look more distinct - as opposed to many girls in the U.S. who are trying to fit into some unspoken, but agreed upon, physical aesthetic of immense boobs and trout-like lips.

Another big factor as to why I enjoy European porn more is that they still give a shit about value and quality. Some companies, like Marc Dorcel and Private, make a concerted effort to film beautiful movies in real locations with an emphasis on production design, costumes and story. They hire good-looking talent and the sex is filmed beautifully.

The other side of that genre is the reality/gonzo style titles shot by the likes of Rocco Siffredi, Manuel Ferrara and Christoph Clark. No story, no elaborate sets, just hot woman fucking. I like that too. They are passionate and nasty with the sex and it tends to be a little more primal.

With the Internet making porn so readily viewable, there is too much bad porn out there. The whole idea of the "girl next door" being in a sex video has given way to amateur shooters and literally the girl next door in front of the camera, who has no idea what sexy is, or how to even make an erotic scene. It has seemingly come down to people just being penetrated with little or no effort on their part to portray the erotic side of sex.

Chapter 57- Do you prefer real breasts or fake breasts?

Of all the questions I have been asked over the years, the one topic that constantly came up were my thoughts on breast enhancement. More and more women are getting their tits done. Even eighteen-year-old girls are getting boob jobs, as if it was some right of passage into adulthood. During my time in the adult film industry I have seen tits of all shapes and sizes; small and flat A's, cute B cups, perky C's, bountiful D's, and much, much bigger sizes.

During my first few months in the business, I remember being hired to do a scene with a girl named Wendy Whoppers who, at the time, had something along the lines of 44 double F sized tits. When I first saw a picture of them, I was a little scared. Her tits were so unnaturally huge and distracting, I was concerned that I wouldn't be able to keep my wood. When I finally did meet her, I found her to be a sweet person with a beautiful slim and fit body. Other than her enormous breasts, she was a normal, attractive girl.

I don't know the reasons for her getting her tits done to that extent, but I suspect it was in order to distinguish herself in the business. She accomplished that and our scene was actually really fun.

I've also had the experience of seeing some of the worst boob jobs out there. Not that they are Frankenstein tits, but I've seen girls settle for procedures from doctors that left horrible scars from the sutures around the areola or long wide scars underneath the breast that were never properly hidden because the implants were too large.

Some girls complained of losing sensitivity in the nipples because of the operations or of being talked into a larger size implants by doctors or boyfriends. Many of these girls would return to work way too soon, and when their breasts finally settled, they just didn't look as good as they may have hoped for.

I've also seen and felt some incredible tits that were implants but were done so well, usually through the armpits, that I couldn't feel the difference. Janine, Racquel Darrian, Asia Carrera, Christine Angel, Dasha and Taylor Hayes all had great fake tits. They looked real and felt tremendous. I would have to say that normally, I favor real breasts to fake breasts.

But if the implants look great, are in proper proportion to the girl's frame, have a minimum of scarring and time is taken to let them heal properly, they are just as nice to look at as natural ones.

Chapter 58- Did you break your penis?

Yes, I did, in fact, break my penis.

My first four years in the business were a busy time for me. Shoot after shoot, my penis went through varying degrees of trauma. Whether being in unusual positions, the angle of penetration being extreme, or just missing the pussy while thrusting, there were many occurrences when damage was inflicted on my little guy.

On at least three different occasions I can recall where, during constant heavy thrusting, I completely missed the opening. In that split second, my fully engorged cock bent at a 90-degree angle. This causes penile fracture and damages the internal tissue of the three chambers that allow the penis to become erect. When this happens, you sometimes hear a pop or cracking sound followed by extreme pain and sometimes a burst blood vessel. Trust me, it fucking hurts!

At the time the damage to my penis wasn't apparent. But when I stopped performing during the course of four years, my penis began to heal internally and that's when the damaged tissue became calcified and scar tissue formed. When the scar tissue begins to form internally, it can prevent the penis from attaining its normal shape when erect. The tissue is now harder and it resists the natural shape when blood enters the chambers. So, when the penis is full and erect, a curve develops.

My curve started out going to the right but for whatever reason when it finished healing, my penis curved upwards like a banana.

This is a condition called Peyronie's. According to medical journals, "it results in the formation of a lump or a scar in the upper or lower layers of the male phallus that contain the erectile tissue leading to the inflammation, irritation and reduction of elasticity of the affected area. This eventually results in bending of the penis during erections as well as pain and emotional distress."

Many girls love the fact that it curves that way because it stimulates their g-spot during intercourse. Before the incident, my penis, being thick and perfectly straight, would hit the cervix bone in many of the girls, which was as painful to them as it was to me. Though it appears that the length is reduced after the curve developed, it just appears that way. The length is still the same but it is no longer in a straight line. If you take two 8 inch pieces of rope, lay it out on a flat surface with one going straight and the other with an upward curve, you can see how one has the illusion of being shorter, when in reality they are both the same length.

On camera a straight cock is easier to shoot as the guy can pull back and forth in long strokes. My curved cock has to fight for camera time.

Chapter 59- Do you think porn will ever be outlawed?

There are many laws that don't allow for the filming of adult films in certain counties or cities in the U.S. At this time of writing, to receive a film permit in Los Angeles, the production is supposed to require the performers to wear condoms. This may drive the business of professional filming away from California and into the hands of people making amateur pornography and releasing it straight to the web.

The porn industry in California is, frankly, on its last legs. It's another industry broken apart by the demand for instant, cheap product and excessive regulations.

Whether by community groups or the shifting tides of economics and market costs, the business may evolve into something else - but I don't believe it will be outlawed. There is too much money to be made by the big communications and media conglomerates and the internet providers who have made access to low cost, low quality pornography as easy as buying a pack of cigarettes.

Chapter 60- What famous celebrities have you met because they were porn fans?

Being an adult film star has definitely presented many situations where famous (and not so famous) celebrities have made it known that they were big fans of mine. Actors, MMA fighters, comedians, rock stars, directors and others have all expressed their love of porn movies, sometimes of a particular role of mine in a feature, or just an overall appreciation (or envy) of my job.

It's a trip when the people I grew up watching on TV or seeing regularly on the big screen recognize me. They come over to introduce themselves and pepper me with questions related to the porn industry. I've actually arranged for some of these celebrities to come to the set when we film; offering them an uncensored view of the reality of making these films.

I remember attending a professional sports game in L.A. where my buddy and I had scored some premium seats. During a timeout, I made my way towards the bathrooms and, as I walked along the railing, I noticed a very famous actor walking towards me.

I had to say something to him-- something along the lines of how much I loved watching his movies and that I thought he was a great actor-- and as he got closer I leaned in towards him and quickly expressed my thoughts. He hurriedly glanced up at me, said thank you and continued on his way. A second later, he paused and slowly turned his head back to me. He looked at me over his glasses and a sly smile appeared on his face. He stepped back towards me and at the same time I sensed people beginning to look at our exchange. A devilish grin made its way to his face as he reached for my hand and with his head tilted back as if to ponder what he would say next, his eyebrows arched, his teeth bared themselves and he chuckled "And I'm a huge fan of your work, Mr. St. Croix."

That moment was probably one of the most memorable that I can remember. It happened out of the blue, by chance. The reason he remembered my name was beyond me but it felt pretty cool to be acknowledged by one of the world's most famous actors.

Chapter 61- Why didn't you become a mainstream actor?

Hollywood is a peculiar business. For actresses who are pretty and want to be considered for serious roles, the men in positions of power almost always want to be rewarded with sex. The women are attractive and the men's desire for them is enhanced because they know that an actress may not have a problem sleeping with someone in order to get the role of their dreams or to jumpstart their career. And if they do end up exchanging sexual favors in order to secure a role, that is considered standard business in Hollywood.

That actress may be considered a "serious actress" but both parties have a lot at stake if anyone said anything so they agree to keep their mouths shut about what happens behind closed doors.

Once you are recognized as being a face and name in the adult business, the roles you get offered dwindle down to porn star roles, hookers, johns or strippers. You're simply not taken seriously as having a skill set in the craft of acting.

The fact is this; network TV shows have advertisers. Those advertisers are typically large corporations and their market is the middle-class American family. They will not risk being taken to task by a group of concerned citizens over the casting of an actor or actress who can be seen on the web engaging in "devious sex acts".

I've had auditions where directors, producers or casting people recognize me and don't even bat an eye. But I've also lost serious consideration for roles because someone recognized me and made a stink about it. There is a lot of rejection that comes with going up for roles in Hollywood and to be honest, I wasn't ready to take that rejection in order to get a small role. Yeah, they say there are no small roles - but believe me, there are. A one-liner as a patrolman will not get you noticed and it will certainly not satisfy your desire to be a thespian.

Although I truly think I have just as much skill as many actors working today in Hollywood, I don't feel the need to prove anyone wrong in their perception of me. They will think what they will think.

If they get a chance to know me personally, they would be very surprised to find out how different I am from the stereotype they may

perceive me to be.

Chapter 62- How do you view your career in adult films now?

It's definitely a mixed bag for me. Having reflected on the choices I've made and the mindset I've operated with when I was young, it sometimes makes me feel sad. I see a young guy who was just as fucked up emotionally as anyone else in the business. I was a broken person who tried to make myself feel better. I thought that sex, money and an easy lifestyle would make me happy in the end.

People say you shouldn't have regrets but I don't agree with that. If you don't feel disappointment about some of the choices and behaviors that led to negative consequences later in life, then how will you know whether you've grown as a human being? What have you learned? What could you offer to someone as advice who may want to get into that business? I would be willing to bet that a majority of the choices we make when we are young and ignorant are based solely on what we feel would give us the most pleasure at the moment with the least amount of work. I feel I have slighted myself by letting these choices be dictated by a warped and immature view of the world.

But I don't think it's healthy to dwell on disappointment. Don't regret the experiences-those experiences shape who you are. That is the fundamental flaw of youth; very rarely can we imagine ourselves twenty years from now. But I also do not dwell in the past. All you have is today. The past is the past and the future is not guaranteed to anyone.

We think of ourselves abstractly. We see ourselves as having, or doing, or being something. But that vision is based upon a premise that we will get whatever we think we deserve. When you're young, you don't think about mortality. But the truth is: what we do now has repercussions further on in life with our family, friends, lovers, employment and social opportunities.

However, I learned more about the true nature of people while working in the industry than I ever would have learned from the church or my family. I learned what the entertainment industry is really all about and I saw the hard reality of life for millions of people.

I've had opportunities to travel the world. I've had leisure time to read and study the things

I found interesting in life. I've had the money to buy trucks, cars and motorcycles that I wanted. I've had the opportunity to donate money to causes I felt were important. I've visited friends and relatives who lived in different parts of the country and the world.

All these things were made possible because of the time and money my work afforded me. I had been raised with a sheltered view of the world and it would have done me more harm than good continuing to live with that limited view.

Given the fact I had no college degree at the time, had I not entered the adult entertainment world, I may have been working low-paying jobs for most of my life. I had no inclination to attend college. I couldn't wait to get out of high school. That's the truth. And with that, I am forever grateful that I have had the career that I've had.

I'd like to think I treated the people I worked in the same way I wanted to be treated, and also made them feel good about themselves. I know I may not have always done that and I have no illusions about the person I was at times. I've said and done things that weren't in line with who I truly am as a person now. There are a lot of people who I still think about to this day because I genuinely liked them. I will always remember them and I wish them success and happiness in their lives after the adult business.

Printed in Great Britain
by Amazon.co.uk, Ltd.,
Marston Gate.